Poetry: A Little of This and Little of That

Poetry: A Little of This and Little of That

Dan E. Blackstone

Copyright © 2018 by Dan E. Blackstone.

ISBN   Softcover   978-1-951469-42-9

All rights reserved. No part of this book may be reproduced or transmitted in any form or by any means, electronic or mechanical, including photocopying, recording, or by any information storage and retrieval system without express written permission from the author, except in the case of brief quotations embodied in critical reviews and certain other non-commercial uses permitted by copyright law.

Printed in the United States of America.

BookWhip
1321 Buchanan Rd.,
Pittsburg, CA 94565

Contents

Nature

Forest Reflections 9
A Winter Thought Of Spring 10-11
The Hay Rake 11
The Grey Menace 12-13
Who Is He 14
Val's Soliloquy 15
That Smell 16
Spring Is Coming 17-18
Blue Trails 18
The Staffers 19-20
The Patio 21
Leaves As Toys 22
August Evening In A Woods 23-24
Autumn Rain 25
Spring Snow And Fog 26-27
April Snow 28-29
Low Tide And Barefoot 30-31
It's Raining Leaves 31
Autumn Serenade 32
The Mighty Swamp Maple 33

Humor

A Stately Maid 37
A Smile 37
Swimming Started With A Splash 38
Amazing 39
Beth's Knee 40
Teeth 41
My Body 42
Problems 43-44
On Xmas Day 44

The Long Wait 45-46
Just A Tree 47
Once Upon A Time 48-49
Moku 50-51
The Tea Party 51
Another April Fool 52
Kermit Was Irish? 53
Winter Weather 54
Fifth Of September 55
So I'm Bald 56
Truth & Consequences 57
Really!? 58
Speed 59
Four Score And Four 59
The Under Taker 60
Was He, Or Wasn't He? 61
Media Emulation 62-63
The Accident 64
The Gift, Tied With A Blue Ribbon 65
One Tiny Cell: The Life Saver 66

Recollections

The Gauntlet 69
Lafayette Street 70
The Hammock 71-72
Church Flowers 73
Cabbage In Refrigerator 74-75
Tire Swing 76
You Can Tell At A Glance 77
The Old Swing Is Gone 78
The Indian Head 79
The Three "e's" 79
Peggy And Friend 80

Tributes

The Souk 83-85
Young Artists 85
My Mother 86
Tin Cans And Battleships 87
Dr. "K" Where Are You? 88-89
I Trod 90-91
The Empty Desk And Vacant Chair 92
Gretel (Marilyn ...) 93-94
Real Dedication And Lack Of It 95-96
Egypt 97-100
Secrets Shared 101
Doctor's Care 102
A Saint 103-104
He Was Seventeen 105-106
An Unknown Hero 107-108
Quite A Guy 108
Devastation 109-110
Heaven Ought To Be 111-112
Solitude 113
Springtime 114
In A Dark Wood 115-116
A Certain Kind Of Freedom 117
Did Anybody Know? 118
His Garden Of Life 119-120
Autumn Year 121
I'm Ninety-Nine 122
The Answers Of A Star 123-124
The Departure 125-126
And I Remembered 127-128
Heavenly Bound 129
Sail On 130-131
The Guiding Hand 132-133
Volunteers 134
Mrs. Pafford's Secret Love 135
This Is My Life 136-137
Gotta Go 'N Sail 138
England To New York 139-140

Philosophy

They Didn't Die 143=144
A Leader 144
Ancestors 145
Eddie's Sweet Shop 146
I May Not Be 147
Two Shadows 148
Labor Day 2002 149
Follow Me 150
Sandy 151-152
The Spirit Of Progress 153
Do I Have To Be Free 154
Unsurpassed Christian 155
Remembrance 156
Look Deeply 157
Sunset Of The Season 158
Stonington Stroll 159
What's There To Complain About 160

Valentines

A Moment 163
Dusting 164
Who Is Most Perfect 165
Emeralds 166
What's Wrong With Society 167
Notes 168-169
Royale Jelly 169
Questions 170
Gratitude 171
Each Day I Give Thanks 172

Barbe

Haircut 175
Come—Walk Along With Me 175
A Kind Lady 176-177
A Rose Among Roses 178
Bridges 179
Music Makers 180
Your Love 180
A Symphony Of Life 181
At The Flood Of Our Lives 182
The Way 183
Your Aura 184
Look For Me 185

Nature

Forest Reflections

I made a forest the other day-
I cut and cleared the brush away,
And let standing slim and fair
Young maples in bright warm air;
Years from now they'll walk this stand
Savoring an autumn of beauty grand
And maybe spy a prancing deer
As it dashes o'er the leaves in fear,
The majestic carpet in rainbow love
Reflecting back to the life above—
Or perhaps a walk in a misty rain
And a melodious sound of drops again
Landing on the chromatic floor
Intensifying glistening colors galore;
And some may pause, meditate and say
What a glorious forest someone has made.

A Winter Thought Of Spring

Browns and Grays and Tans
Rustle from the winds' pressure.
Here and there a squeak or creak
As two trees rub, or bend too far;
A rattling sound or crunching
As leaves scamper over one another
In their rush to pile up as energy producers.
Such is the sight on this brisk wintry day
In the sunlit woods that overlooks a glen.
Soon the colors will change to a budding red,
A cherry-like color ranging from deep maroon
To a brighter strawberry hue;
Change from brown to chartreuse,
Change from tan to a lemon yellow,
Change from gray to green.
This transformation sounds the alarm
That spring is about to dress in all her finery,
That she will cast off the dull and will vividly
Burst forth in her nuptial splendor,
Signaling to all the warmth of love.
The stonewall, hidden in summer,
Is stark but beautiful bathed with sunlight.
The lichen-green is almost opalescent
Reflecting the mixture of yellowish sun rays,
Emphasizing the dark shadows of rock spaces.
The leaf carpet reflects every shade of brown and tan.
Many of the trees reflect the same colors of the gray-green wall,
Even to the upper branches encrusted in lichens.
Life is at a standstill:
Waiting for the glory of light;
Waiting for the lengthening of daylight;
Waiting for the warmer days;
Waiting for the thunder and rain.

But for now, the wind blows,
Disconnecting the dead branches,
Disconnecting the leaves that cling from last year,
Disconnecting the trees from long ago useless roots.
Just cleansing the forest, sweeping the landscape,
Preparing for spring in her array
Of color and newness and love.

The Hay Rake

There's a place I know well
With memories fond and dear,
Where the climate and the smell,
Varies, and the work severe.
The hay rake sits in the Autumn sun,
No longer needed, its work is done;
The days grow shorter, the nights are calm,
It's no longer needed on the Hanover farm.
But the owner left all that behind,
He'd rather travel through frontiers of time,
From the south to the Alaskan border he explored,
From East to West, adventures galore!
Now years later he still likes to roam,
And it's hard to tell, where he calls home,
And there's no use to stifle his noble pride,
He'll kick it loose, so long as he can ride.
Now, the hay rake sits idle, alone,
Waiting for its master to return home.

The Grey Menace

Daring, defiant, sassy, a real adventurous sort,
Has no regard for property and brazen with his "torts;"
Into densest forest or into your yard he'll come
Searching for free handouts, any kind of crumb.
With leaps and bounds he'll traverse a field,
He openly scampers with nerves of steel:
Climbing a tree is no trouble at all
He does it all year, spring, summer, winter and fall.
Agility and balance are built into this guy,
No shrub too low, no tree too high;
A model of coolness as he sits and chatters,
He'll even scold when no food's on the platter.
He ransacks bird feeders with insolent bobbing,
And snorts at attempts toward stopping his robbing.
When two or more of these little rascals
Clamor together they start to "wrassel,"
Then a delightful display of leaps and bounds
From tree to tree, then along the ground;
Then up to the fence and along its top,
They balance themselves and never stop:
Until one slows and the other leaps over
And the race is on as fast as a plover,
And just as fast with gymnastic flair
From branch to branch they flit through the air.
A dog penned below looks up with disdain
As these two taut him and tease without shame.
His barking and running to and fro
Encourages antics and a spiteful show,
Then away again in mock aerial combat
No hesitation . . . a constant attack!!

Then it's time again to go and feed,
The birds care not and there's an energy need.
Stuffing themselves while they incessantly search
For food in the feeder and down on the earth,
Then back to the trees these dare-devil imps
Fearlessly climbing, from no danger they shrink,
Tumbling, rumbling, with spinning and swirl
That's *Scurius carolinensis*, our little gray squirrel!!

Who Is He?

He scurried over the walls in the shade or in the sun,
He scurried along the ground ... my ... he was so full of fun!
He jumped a mighty jump for one so tiny and quick
From the ground back to the wall he went, lickity—split.
He flitted along stuffing his cheeks with all that he could carry,
Then back to his den with his food ... no time to tarry.
From early spring you'll find him quickly going about
On through the summer he runs ... that's why he isn't stout.
Then during the fall he begins his serious scoot
For food like seeds, acorns, and even types of roots.
He stores up food in various ways and in nearby dens,
All the while his business leaves him with very few friends!
You may see him on a tree stump in weather that is fair
But when he runs, he runs with his tail straight in the air.
And sometimes in his travels if he openly sits and gawks,
He may meet with danger such as a sharp eyed hawks!
So he doesn't get much pleasure by sitting in the sun,
Although he may like it, it's safer on the run:
You cannot leave your food in a car with windows cracked
For he'll smell it out and you'll find no lunch when you get back!
He's called a lot of things in different parts of the world
But his actions are the same no matter where he whorls ....
He's happy while he's working, not looking for any fame,
He doesn't even know he has a very special name:
Some people call him one thing, some people call him another,
But to scientific people, *Tamias striatis* is his cover!!

Val's Soliloquy

I think that I shall never see
A car that's stronger than a tree,
A mighty tree that sometimes wears,
Fenders or bumpers in its hair;
A tree is always in one place,
It doesn't move or change its pace.
A car you must always steer
Should you come upon a deer!
Those cute bambyites with night vision
Who seldom ever have a night collision!
But on occasion in their line of sight
Comes a speeder with very bright, bright lights,
Blinding their chosen path so free
Causing them to snag a tree!
Or if the car is of the smaller brand,
The deer may stop and take a stand,
The car hits it and there's no contest,
The car stops running, it's quite a mess!
The deer then quietly walks without grief
While the driver sits in sad disbelief,
Looking at the crinkled metal,
Watched the dust begin to settle.
The deer has disappeared among the trees
And the driver sits in the cool night breeze,
Contemplating a brand new meaning
Of understanding over-breeding!
It matters not what the cost,
The car is such a total loss,
Just send the bill to the 'animal league'
And while at it, mention the disease
That deer transport to make humans sick
All this done via the little deer tick!
Ah yes, it matters not how straight the way
Or whether it's night or whether it's day,
Steer your car, when out on a spree,
Away from a deer, hit a Tree!!

That Smell

Marmota monox is daring today
   As he steals across the lawn.
His smeller must be leading the way,
   Heedless to the passing storm.
What delectable odor wafts the breeze
   To make him leave his home?
And stealthily creep and suddenly freeze
   To the strangeness as he roams.
Look how brave is this cheeky rover
   Searching the green strewn yard,
For flowering rain washed clover
   Blossoming in the lawn-like sod.
He inches ahead, stops and looks about,
   Then continues on with his task;
Ever ready for a sudden rout
   From any attackers dash!
But the plucky adventurer has found his trove
   Of droplet ridden clover,
And he is deeply indebted to his nose
   For the tantalizing trip is over!

Spring Is Coming

Mephitis mephitis is hungry
    and it's easy for me to tell,
He's left his den to search for food,
    this I know from his smell.
Winter has been long and the ground
    stays covered with snow,
And poor Mephitis is missing
    his mid-winter snack, I know.
He's out there foraging for food
    of any type or sort
And he isn't fussy or finicky,
    that seems to be the report.
Even in town I smelled him
    and I know that he was there
For my eyes were burning and stinging
    from the heavy ladened air.
Now this fine looking species
    in his tenacious search and drive
Doesn't usually leave his den
    'til just before spring arrives.
Although his clock may tell him
    that it's now wake-up time,
Mother Nature seems to be late
    and a little bit behind:
For she has painted all the landscape,
    in the period of one night,
And she's done it very quickly
    in tones of black and white.
Now this could be misconstrued
    as a tribute to our hungry friend
Because you see with his colors
    into this scene he'd easily blend.
Mephitis is not easily frightened
    as he makes his hungry rounds,

And he could become a regular,
   if your trash can abounds.
He'll eat from your hand
   if you take time and do not blink
But for goodness sake don't startle him
   or pungently you'll stink!
Should you mistakenly and suddenly
   incur his protective wrath,
Keep on hand tomato juice
   to take with you to your bath.
You may think it's unusual
   to bathe with this kind of junk,
But you'll find it really works
   if you unexpectedly meet a SKUNK!!

Blue Trails

Blue trails lead to prizes so adored,
Trace them to the mountain tops L'Amour.
Inch by inch to the peaks so pert,
Vicarious feelings keeps one alert.
Those trails are purposely colored blue,
Easy to follow, encouraging you.
So enjoy each curve and vista smooth,
An exotic choice for you to choose;
Give thanks to the creation of trails so nice,
Give thanks not once, but do it twice!
Praises be you reached the peaks so fair,
Now relax, enjoy your moments there.

THE STAFFERS

They are gathering by the hundreds
    Even thousands some will say-
They are gathering in the sunshine
    At the very break of day.
They are sitting there and resting
    After an early morning spree-
They remained alone in darkness
    Or in groups of two or three
And the hunger that develops
    After fasting all the night
Causes everyone to waken
    And lift in searching flight.
They were swooping down and turning
    Catching insects on the wing;
They were very acrobatic while
    Doing their breakfast thing.
Now is the time for resting
    And gossiping's begun,
No need to keep on flying
    When you can bask right in the sun.
As they sit with equal spacing
    And preen and peck and sass
It looks more like an orchestra
    Or giant music staff!
The director's not arrived yet
    They are just now tuning up,
Soon they'll leave in loops and dives
    And return in time to sup.
I don't know why or what
    Such a gathering's all about,
Could it possibly be they're
    Planning their trip on to the south?
It's the last week in August
    And at least a month to go

There's plenty of time for planning
    Even if some are slow!
But look again at the spacing,
    And the sagging of the line,
Does it remind you of music?
    two four or four four time?
Listen to the music
    As it ascends and descends the staff,
Listen to the music
    As it stimulates a laugh.
I can imagine this music
    Going up and down the scale
In harmonic triads
    Or dissident off key wails:
But as I see the notes
    Against the royal blue,
It reads as an opera aria
    Not off key, but true!
Something just sounds majestic
    And pleasant to follow,
As we silently listen
    To these gregarious swallows.

The Patio

It's warm-
The birds are singing
The insects and bees are buzzing
But the air is still—sort of tranquilized -
The blossoms soundlessly are bursting
Adding to the wonderment of nature.
A dog barks and races through the field-
But not disturbing the natural battle.
An odd smell, not unpleasant permeates the air-
The brightness is almost blinding
As the sun reflects from the dew and mist-
A pair of robins appear, ignoring your intrusion
And nonchalantly eke out their existence.
He's back—silent, wet, panting, snooping and happy-
A hint of a breeze reports another strange aroma;
Pleasing-
Suddenly all is changed, a cloud screens
Out the warmth and brightness-
Now the lonely seeding dandelion loses its majestic halo,
And seems strange and silent and out of place.
Suddenly you hear a loud pleasant throaty sound;
Then an oriole swoops low- skipping over
The grass bending from beads of sequins
And then rises into the branches studded with blossoms
Soon to be apples:
The sun is higher now—the clouds have passed;
It's warm.

Leaves As Toys

Mariah has swirled all the leaves last night
In rows and piles with colors bright,
This deed was done
And to the horror of some
It made them weary and rather numb!
For leaves from yards were piled in another,
To owners who had raked, and cleaned the cover;
And along the streets in some small towns,
Long rows of leaves to leeward are found!
The complaints are loud by grumbling sages,
You hear in their whining and tell from their phrases.
They have no recollection of the beautiful sights
Or they'd stop the grumbling and listen to delights;
Hear that rustling and screams of excitement,
As children scatter the knee-deep enticement
Joyously rolling, jumping and shuffling through rows
For that is the real reason the old wind blows!
To hear that rustling, scampering, of loves and joys,
Leaves piles high make wonderful toys!

August Evening In A Woods

Melodious, throaty sounds break the solitude of silence
As a Warbler talks to the setting sun in gratitude.
Looking up toward the eastern forests the sun
Paints a yellowish tinge to the green as it touches the blue;
There are hints of white veils filtering the light, and
Reflecting the blue in different shades.
No leaves rustle,
No branches move,
No air currents,
So the sounds seem to drop down around you,
Absorbed by the trees; the ground cover seems to bounce
The sound back, making it difficult to locate their origins.
A twitter from the distance, another call as though in
Answer to the Warbler, who continues its whistle-like
Throaty tune of thanks for an almost perfect day.
Blue Jays call an answer in their goodnight serenade.
The beech tree looks grand, glorious and clean
Contrasting its yellowish green terminus from the sun,
To the darker green leaves in shadow on the lower branches.
The joyous sounds have decreased. In the far distance
Is the barely audible sound of a murder of crows,
As they ready for the night's coolness, which now envelopes one.
There is a suggestion of a breeze
As one watches the lower branches of the beech.
In the pine, the sun reflects golden copper brown
Emphasizing those needles ready to be shed,
In order to add to the matte cover around the trunk.
There in the old stark tree standing by the wall,
A tree that has not borne leaves in many years,
A tree that has been bleached gray for eons,
Sits a hawk looking over its domain:
The forest floor is silent—he might as well go home.

And the birds in their melodious salute to the day
Have reduced their chorus to a quartet or two—
Most of the trees are a contrast of dark green beneath a veil of blue,
With a few of the tallest bathed in sunlight.
Now, the solitary Warbler is back to its perch, not singing-
As the silence becomes more intense.
Soon the night sounds will commence,
And the August evening will be bathed in starlight,
Deep blue and night.

Autumn Rain

Walking in a light intermittent *Autumn Rain*
Silently, amidst the brilliant hues,
I step upon a carpeted lane,
Reflecting the sunspots passing through.

No fear here of getting wet,
Rainbow umbrellas encircle one as a sheath;
The rain falls from where it was set,
In the form of a multicolored leaf.

They encompass me as a cloak,
Lightly falling to the earth,
Allowing children or older folk,
To shuffle through with exuberant mirth.

Soon, this pleasure so keen and clean,
Will only be a reflected memory;
The carpet will not be seen,
No one will know of this revelry

Or that once a multi colored path,
Lay there as a vibrant lane,
Deposited there by a lovely,
Light, intermittent *Autumn Rain*.

Spring Snow and Fog

The mystical gray obliterates the landscape.
It surrounds me closer than a woolen cape:
Yet, I cannot touch this ominous frock
In this early hour at five of the clock!
I know the ground is covered with snow
It is barely visible as I glance below.
As the clock moves on with relentless stride,
Darkness and invisibleness begin to subside.
White ground seems to materialize so pale,
Visible a few yards, then a milky veil,
Which rises up and covers the sky
And comes down again on the other side-
I am enveloped by this hemispherical display
That magically transforms from white to gray.
How beautiful and yet so drab, dull, and numb
Standing alone it seems almost sad and glum.
There is a silent peaceful interlude
In this private grayish solitude-
I knew what should be there outside this limited finiteness
And I strain to see the hidden enshrouded objects of 'familiarness':
No movement of air, no swirling currents or sign of day,
Just suspended visible yet untouchable matrix of gray.
No sound disturbing the eerie yet deafening silent collection,
If a sound occurs, it descends without identifiable direction.
In a mesmerized trance,
I stare to see any familiar objects at all
And my imaginative mind says, yes,
There is a tree and a wall;
Then my concentration increases and I take a stance,
There is no object there, it's just my mental trance.
I must wait for passing time; it is my decision,
With increasing light will come better vision.
Then, in the white-grayish gloom I deduce

My world of limited sight is clearer, not reduced:
There before me lies one,
No two features recognized with glee;
One is the snow drifted wall, the other, a pine tree.
There! A movement in this days dim lighted birth,
A bird silently glides into view, down to earth:
Having safely navigated with uncanny skill and sight,
The solemn silver-ish grayness and dangers of blind flight.
Amazing! It knows where it is in this fog!
How is its height known above this white-gray sod?
My mind is inundated with questions and wonder at mother nature's plan
When I witness this silent phantom-glider appearing so magically to land.
The bird sees me and without sound rises up to instantly disappear,
Again I wonder how this aviator knows where to steer.
Intently I strain to see the angle of flight,
But all I see is a brightening dome of white.
All life is like this—we appear out of dark concealment,
And feel our way into a panacea of enlightenment,
And rise up to unlimited heights and visions of love
Emancipated from the dark,
The gray, to brightness above!
The world is becoming visible as I look across the field;
Those stratified layers of fog with light are being annealed
And I am back again in the familiar and the bold . . . .
It's time for me to go inside, so my story can be told.

April Snow

It's April first, and snowing: a pleasant sort of snow.
The temperature is in the high thirties
And daffodils are in bloom-
What an inspiring sight,
Especially with crocus
Nodding and
Coloring to
Natures
Numbers

Snow lands lightly on the windscreen
And for a split second its
Design enchants one,
It seems to curl up,
then Slowly it
dissipates to
a drop of
water;
Nature
At
Play.

It's intriguing to sit and watch the many various
Trees, flowers, lawns and ponds disappear
As though a hazy Curtain envelops
Everything obliterating your
Vision of distant objects that
Nature has only moments
Before displayed with
Brilliant vividness
To lift spirits
And please
And
Love.

Poetry: A Little of This and Little of That

This is an example of trust and belief,
For you know beauty was there
And trust it will be there again
When the curtain rises
Justifying your firm
Belief in Nature
Reinforcing
Your faith
In
Man.
Now the glass is dotted with diamonds
Reflecting light adding to the curtain
And mystifying the scene of the
Lightly twisting falling snow
That swirls and dims the
glorious distant objects.
Then the sun tries
To burst through
And spotlight
The daffodils
And crocus
so
Blue.
It's as though Nature is saying, here I am
On the rise, here I am justifying life,
Here I am, a monument to love
Of beauty; then the clouds
thicken and the veil is
back as we try and
locate the haloed
monument to
Nature on
This first
of April
in the
Pleasant
Sort
Of
Snow.

Low Tide And Barefoot

Ten or eleven, the age to be,
Foot loose and fancy free;
Barefoot at the shore he stands
Squiggling toes into the sand.
Then wading with water to his knees,
Climbed a rock enshrouded in seaweed.
A ballet he then did perform,
As from rock to rock he balanced long.
Squatting, into the deeper water gazed
Into the clear pool he stared amazed!
Heeding not the slippery mess,
Nor the barnacles that tear the flesh;
His soul and soles protectively encased,
Belief in Nature is what a boy's life is laced;
Then from rock to rock he danced again,
Back to shore where his shoes have lain.
Spying a barnacled piling standing free,
A remnant of a dock from a raging sea-
He carefully avoided a sharp shelled path
And ventured to examine the stele shaft,
Where once boats moored near a protective spit,
But in one raging hurricane the piling split.
Partially buried in sand and mud and rock,
Were timbers that once formed a sturdy dock.
An eel, a crab, moved to the marine grass,
Cautiously they moved to the concealing mass.
As he with equally cautioned moves
Investigated the enticing growth in grooves.
Squatting to watch the enthralling plants,
A turbulent rogue wave soaked his once dry pants.
There, a starfish in a feeding mood,
Slowly moved to the mussel food!
He watched the hundreds of feet attack,
The mussel opened to provide a snack.

Then with wet clothes another sight,
On the beach rose hips, a sweet delight.
In his rush to feed he stubbed his toe,
Then stepped on a briar adding to his woe.
But barefoot boys often with this stuff collide,
After a hip or two the pain did subside.
Tough feet are normal for a barefoot boy, (girl)
Let nothing deter your low tide joy. (world)

It's Raining Leaves

It's raining leaves today
Fall is definitely under way,
The colorful maples with leaves so gay
Are covering the ground in great array.
After a week or more we'll gladly say,
Let's walk the painted pastel display
Reflecting so brilliantly the sunny rays!
Not a deluge by any means,
But a sort of tree by tree, steady stream,
Of Nature preparing the disrobing scheme,
Preparing for the winter scene,
With the howling winds that it does bring!
But let's not speak of a dismal thing,
Enjoy the rainbow so enlightening,
Think on how joyful church bells ring
As you stroll and scuff the leafy path
In hiking boots and sturdy staff!

Autumn Serenade

Does music really set your mind
    to a wandering dreamy state?
Does it get right down inside you
    and increase the heartbeat rate?
Is there a whelming of elation
    as you burst forth into song?
Is there a warm and cheery feeling
    in seeing the righting of some wrong?
Oh there's a joyous, religious beaming
    just aching for release,
It's a melodious rapturous reasoning
    to put the world at peace.
And scenes of pastoral splendor
    parade before your eyes
In an endless chromatic rainbow
    as an autumn painter's pride.
You can feel the tune's excitement
    as a September serenade
Passes on into October
    and the leaves reduce their shade;
And the colors all are falling
    in a soft, almost silent sound,
Then a gentle breeze entangles
    the colors on the ground;
Reflecting back the music
    in a scampering, trilling race,
Swelling with shifting colors
    the crescendo now takes place.
Then, a solitary leaf flutters
    from the place where it was hooked,
And lands without a splash
    in the slowly moving brook.
There, resounding with many others
    in a harmonious, colorful ring,
The symphony now starts all over,
    with a whole rest 'til it's spring.

The Mighty Swamp Maple

It stood in the swamp, sturdy and strong;
Massive compared to the shrubs that surround.
Stark, silvery grey in reflecting sunlight;
All branches at characteristic divergences,
Enhancing its towering might amidst the lesser.
How stalwart it looked after a winter snow.

Tonight it would be covered due to a pending storm.
Its limbs with white would again abound.
Majestically it's geometric designs will show might!
Crisp, clear, as an inspiring emergence.
It speaks, "I'm crowned, a superb dresser,
Especially after the storm, I'll be best of show!"

It's not there! A blizzard proved it wrong!
There it lies half on the ground,
Reflecting is the splintered trunk of yellowish-white,
As though it went through submergence!
Once it stood as a protector, a 'blesser,'
Now, as firewood will be its only glow!

Humor

A Stately Maid

Stately stands the slender maid,
Lithe and regal she's unafraid;
Assuredly she greets all she meets,
With an inviting manner mild and sweet.
Her smile and pleasant personality
Invigorates the inner spirit exponentially!
All senses surface and admirably swell,
In response to this intriguing belle;
With wholesome manner and pride she stands,
A worthwhile bride for a deserving man.

A Smile

A smile so genuine and full of glee
Spreads across the knowing face so free,
The world should witness this innocent lark
Who holds secret happy knowledge within her heart.

Swimming Started With A Splash

Swimming was learned at an early age,
In a river either at high or lowly stage;
The river allowed activities of all sorts,
And carried no prejudiced, evil thoughts.

Boats, barges, ferries, tugs and more,
She carried them all, not keeping score;
Floating objects were carried through,
Numerous sources contributed (sewers too!).

When we learned to swim the Australian crawl,
(Then it was the overhand stroke, so called)
It was best to splash your hand, you see,
To push aside the odiferous floating debris!

Better that than meeting an object vile,
That could often be smelled for over a mile!
So splash we did as we pulled along,
At also it made our arms real strong!

Amazing

Amazing Grace where art thou now,
I've fed the goat; I've fed the cow;
While you're in the loft upon the hay,
Entertaining for miniscule pay.

Oh amazing Grace tell me nice,
Why with me you double the price?
I've tried and tried to share your space,
But you always treat me with disgrace.

It's really amazing how you hide,
While allowing others to share your side;
But Jesus knows you're like Magdalene,
Serving others on a heavenly scheme.

I guess it's best to go and pray
For your soul as you go and play,
As for me, I'll adjust to the hazing,
How you do it is simply amazing!

Beth's Knee

My daughter's knee is interesting,
   Ask her, she'll tell you so
Her mother always said t'was true
   Of course she ought to know
She bathed her since infancy and some
   Spots more firmly had to rub
Until one day it dawned on her
   That's a birthmark she tried to scrub!
And even so into adulthood
   And after marriage vows
From across the room she'd plainly see
   And with precision she'd announce
Inquisitively What's that dirt there
   I plainly see upon you knee?
Or on occasion would remark
   On your knee I see a smudge.
No- don't you remember mom,
   It's my birthmark so well scrubbed!
You scrubbed it when I was a baby,
You scrubbed when I was a child
   No matter what I said
   You washed for quite awhile.
You scrubbed in pre-adolescence
   When I scraped my knee
And always wondered why
   You had a dislike for me!
Now I am a mother
   And still can't seem to believe
Deep in your heart you still think
   That there is dirt upon my knee!

TEETH

A Dentist is a person adept at accomplishing compassionate feats,
He's a specialist at repairing someone else's teeth;
Modern equipment and painless drilling,
Makes a pained visit a little more willing.
Years ago, like sixty or eighty, or a hundred or so,
A visit to those quacks took lots of courage to go!
Back then a toothbrush was an unheard of item,
And teeth were good for Knorrin' and bittin';
And cleaning teeth was sort of impromtude,
Done through eat'n and chompin' on hard raw food:
So when did the brush make its entrance?
And that other stringy stuff of painful penitance.
Tooth picks were once the point of a knife,
Now they are slender and pointy and white.
But brushes came along some time ago too,
Its greatest impact was during W.W.II.
Right after the depression when teeth were rotten'.
For during that time, t'was cheaper to pull 'em.
T'was a time when cavities were a part of life's frame,
Money was scarce; you tolerated the pain;
Many a child lost molars by the ton,
Teeth rotted off right down to the gum!
Mom's teeth were so painful and she full of agonies,
They calculated the cost to repair those cavities,
Took gas and removed them all from her gums,
Did this with six kids at age 31!
And service dentists removed rotted off teeth 'en Masse'
By simply pryin' 'em with a lever, not any gas!
Nothin' ya said made any difference,
Out they came with little resistance.
Without novocaine they drilled and they drilled,
Then packed 'em with stuff until all were filled.
Sent cha away bravely hoppin' and stompin'
An' said for a day don't do heavy chompin'.
So Dentist are adept at making a life sunny,
But it's done by taking all of your money!!

My Body

My body doesn't like me anymore,
It mentioned it in fevers and much more:
Literally shook me to the very bone
In a vibrant relentless kinda tone;
It took away my tan and color mellow,
Turned me to a ghastly shade of yellow!
Just when I thought I was all set,
Shake some more and then begin to sweat!
I don't mind swimming in warm water
But in bed one really shouldn't—oughter.
The sheets get sticky and pajama's too
Then it's time to head right for the loo!
Disorientation, get thee behind-
Leave me, don't confuse or be unkind!
Now which way was it to the john?
This is urgent: was it thither or yon?
A meandering trip, the bare feet kind,
Pure "Will Power," made it just in time!
(Don't ask which was the greater need,
Just sat and both took heed.)
Oh, where is it aching? Here or there?
Neither, neither, it's everywhere.
The doctors say the medications they're giving
Are just so I could pretend that I'm living.
So I asked the doctors if they'd please
Tell me the name of this disease!
Their answer surprised this cogitative bore;
It's just that your body doesn't like you anymore!!

Problems

Whenever I have a problem
I try to hide the thing:
But there is a limit to the masking,
The inner side does sting.
It's something that just seems to grow
And rise like the dawning sun
It runs right through my body,
Even though nothing's said or done.
The body just responds,
And says a lot of things,
It seems to shout and yell
And warning bells do ring!
And someone asks a question,
"Are you feeling quite all right?"
So the body has said something,
I must be quite a sight!
How the lying, cheating body
Could do such a task,
To tell the world my problem;
It didn't even ask!
Then, maybe its not the body
Who is telling all the stuff,
Maybe it's really the person
Who can read you in the rough.
Trying to be helpful,
That's really not a crime;
It's just the love concern
To keep one in their prime.
There is no major problem
That can't be sent away,
But there always is a chance
It'll come back some other day.

But for this, there is,
A consolation prize,
The intensity reduces,
The mountain is down sized.
With each subsequent revival
Of a similar thought produced,
The body has adjusted
And the pain is now reduced.
So whenever I have a problem
That clutters up my day,
I skip the in between steps
And send it far away!

On Xmas Day

On Xmas day the thunder came
A rumbling through the hillside,
The rain and snow also came
A rumbling through the hillside.
It mattered not to the gathering there,
As it rumbled through the hillside.
The family smiled and played a game
As it rumbled through the hillside.
'Tis Xmas day, they all declared
As it rumbled through the hillside;
Be thankful that the house is warm,
There's no rumbling on the inside!

The Long Wait

While waiting in the doctor's office,
Now that's an understatement
To be examined in some way,
Obvious humor is quite evident
You suddenly realize dignity
And it alleviates the tension
And humility are not in sight that day.
Hopeful smiles reduce resentment.

And it's not a gradual
Then it's finally your turn
Weaning to which you are exposed,
You enter that freezing cell;
While the patient softly speaks
With a paper 'night' shirt
The staff loudly says 'disrobe'!
There's a desire to rebel!

There are no preliminaries,
You vibrate there from head to toe,
No secretiveness in here.
Enter a brazen nurse so bold;
The staff just bellows out
She disgustingly shakes her head
In tones most like a jeer.
En sez, "Are you cold?"

Forms are given to be filled out
In her hand there's a glass rod,
Your cards are taken to copy
So your lips open wide;
They think the numbers are in your brain,
But she's more interested
As on a computer floppy!
In the end you're trying to hide.

Now no one ever tells you
These people are so unpredictable,
To return forms right away,
But merriment prevails
Minutes pass, they call your name
To them it's like you're dancing
"We've' been waiting," they do say!!
The dance of the seven veils!

So you sit another hour
Eventually the doctor comes
While patients come and go;
And probes you here and there,
Hunger pangs are evident,
Then comes the longest moment
How come they are so slow?
While your derriere's in mid-air!

They schedule several patients
Are you married, doctor,
For the identical time slot,
I know this isn't much,
In any other business
But I certainly hope with her
They'd be a starving lot!
You have a gentler touch!

One in four has humor,
Then comes the command
Some intellect and is kind;
You have longed to hear
She informs the waiting invalids
Okay, you can dress now
That they are well behind.
And come again next year!
Confused? Read every other line.

JUST A TREE

How strong and straight the tree stands near,
Its limbs spread o'er a wreck of smear;
   Standing firm on its domain,
   Defying those with little brains,
Who think that their power is a racing spree
But they can't compare with one strong tree.

It doesn't move, it doesn't sway,
It doesn't talk, got nothing to say;
   It need not travel very far,
   Like others in a speeding car;
It just grows old and very strong,
And wakens with the birds at dawn.

So if you think you're smart and brave,
Remember those who're in their grave,
   After whipping along on racing tires
   Never realizing that their new bier,
Could be made from one strong tree,
Perhaps the tree that stopped their spree!

Once Upon A Time

There once was a guy named Reiker
Who was a mail man striker.
He'd go to the town,
In a truck grey, not brown
Saw a girl and said, gosh, I do like her.

He returned every day it is said,
For mail with his hair sorta red,
She winked at him there
He floated on air,
Never thinkin' to her he'd be wed.

From the first time that he appeared
She carefully readied cupids spear,
At his heart she did aim
But inexperience she did blame,
When it hit him square in the rear.

But the prize that was sought
Came about with quick thought
And the voices did sing
Said he'd give her a ring,
It was then she knew he'd been caught.

The story goes on now you see,
A couple first, then it was three;
He took her up North,
Some say by force,
But it was love that made them so free.

And the years they did fly
As she cooked for her guy,
The story they tell
Is he ate all too well,
So bigger pants he had to buy.

Yes the years have moved on
But lost none of the charm
She trained him real good
And leashed where he stood
So he would be safe from all harm.

So the days have flown right along
And they're still singing the same old song,
We have to be thankful
That Bob is so bashful
And that he is seldom ever forlorn.

The secret is to strive
To give each love with pride
If you keep the faith
Trust always your mate
You too can be wed sixty-five.

Moku

He chased the crumpled ball of paper
    and fetched it back to me-
Then bounded again upon the prize
    in a blur of youthful glee,
Then cuffed it back and forth,
    then dropped it for me to see;
In youth he scooted up a limb,
    and had to be retrieved-
Then lost his climbing tines,
    to save the furniture you see!
T'was a sorry sight to witness,
    when he couldn't claw a tree.
Time went on for Moku,
    as it does for all who breathe,
He's moved to another state
    and chases birds and bees,
And stalks on through the woods
    noiselessly on fallen leaves.
He sits and watches the birds above
    as they glide upon the breeze
Taunting him and mocking him,
    oh they're such a tease!
Occasionally he catches one
    and like a fisherman at sea,
He releases it cause it's so small
    plus his teeth aren't what they used to be.
The woods are full of creatures
    from which he cannot flee,
The defensive claws are not there,
    so cautiously he does proceed.
His curiosity is still present
    On jaunts he does spree,
And on occasion he meets a stranger
    who doesn't like his breed,
Though it might be Moku's territory,
    he comes home where he can bleed.

Moku didn't come home last night,
    when called he didn't come to me,
Memories of his independence,
    came flooding back you see,
As he chased a crumpled ball of paper
    and fetched it back to me-
Then bounced again upon the prize
    in a blur of youthful glee.

The Tea Party

Must have a Tea Party, so as to sort things out;
We've got to convince people to get out there and shout!
It matters not how they,
Feel about what politicians say:
We have to wait and see,
What happens at the 'Tea'.
The government supports this group,
As it participates with our troops,
And Congress comes from miles round,
When the location of the party's finally found!
Especially since they now know, you see,
That Tequila's referred to as a Southern TEA.

Another April Fool

(A Silly analogy of some sort)

Seven rhymes with heaven,
  An imaginary haven;
It also rhymes with 'leaven',
  That's bread before it's 'raisin'.

If you look at the number zero,
  There's nothing to brag about,
Unless you think of Nero,
  With him there was a 'FIRE' shout!

Putting them together, side by side,
  You find it's a very pleasant sound.
Not the zero first, don't be snide,
  The seven's first, the other way around.

Seven-zero is really Kool,
  So let's have a little toast,
If they were born an April Fool,
  Some people will even boast!

Here's to the number Seven,
Here's to the Zero Fair,
Here's to a place called Heaven,
But for now, let's not go there.

Kermit Was Irish?

Kermit wasn't always thought to be Irish-
He was there before his color was stylish.
Once he was a ghastly shade of white,
Visibly outstanding, quite a sight!
White on black, a contrasting clash,
Black on white, so blasé, so rash;
There was really not a need for pride,
And no place to really go 'n hide.
Then a slow evolutionary change was seen,
He metamorphosed to a multicolored green!
So clever was his motley colored skin,
That even Humans wished that they was Him!
They thought his color was quite stylish,
Then people called themselves "The Irish".
Decided that Green was a color to be all over,
Especially in the shape of a 4 leaf clover.

Winter Weather

Oh dismal rain, eraser of snow and slush,
Why bring forth the dank so slowly, why not rush?
It's disdainful to maintain a miserable February,
After such a cold and cruel January!
So brutal when driven by the wind and cold,
So baneful, deceptive, especially for the very old.
Return when the flowers need their drink,
Return in Spring to keeping the Rhododendron pink.
Then descend light and gentle over all,
Keeping and feeding so grass grows tall.
Lifting spirits, cleansing the atmosphere,
Giving us comfort without any fear,
But for now, oh demon mean and wet,
Go! Give me warmth, let me sweat!

Fifth of September

(No, I don't know the whiskey company that makes it)

This the fifth of September, 2010,
A day to remember the world of great men!
Now one of these guys, who's still kinda spry,
They say that he'll live, 'til the day that he dies!
It's said that he's now eight plus times ten,
I wouldn't believe it, 'tis true, sez uh friend.
We can verify that fact, it's not a secret well kept,
And his health is measured by his dance-like quick step.
What-ever his age, it ain't really the case,
Though he's older than he's younger of face!
(This author was taught at an early age,
To respect his elder, 'specially this Sage.)
So anniversary greetings to the older in town,
The more you have, the longer you're 'round!
    (from the youthful, debonair, off key tenor who
    respectfully submits this to the Old ON key tenor.)

So, I'm Bald!

Over the years, bald headed men have had to endure
    Comments that men of lesser character couldn't stand,
"Moss doesn't grow on a busy street,"
    a statement not so true;
    For between the bricks it grows
    on highways in" ole Holland!"
"What happened to the wavy hair you had in your youth?"
    "Tis a question often asked in a smirking jibe,
And you must answer and tell the dreadful truth,
    "It didn't like certain people,
    so it really WAVED good-bye."
But someone comes to the defense
    with a friendly sort of fun
    To utterances of "Herr Baron cranium,"
    or a comment not so rare,
When responding to "Help, I'm blinded by reflected sun"!
    It's said, "Your head resembles heaven,
    for there is no parting there!"
Other astute reactions must be conjured on the scene,
    To "Hey, chrome dome" or "What's the time, shine"?!
There may be some answers that reign supreme,
    What kind of brain requires reason to this rhyme?
Then in a flash a phrase from the bible,
    About the sins being as the number of hairs to win
Making such a quote is free of libel,
    My hair number's so small, I'm free of sin!!!

TRUTH & CONSEQUENCES

There is a truism that no one can change
It silently controls us, but we're not to blame.
Each day we use it, heedless, yet sublime,
It has many names but we call it TIME!
As I see it, it is really only a loan;
Some use it wisely, others groan and moan.
Because of miscalculation or without any thought,
They freely waste and 'do not what they ought'.
With each minute, each hour, each day,
Whether at work or whether at play,
Wisely use the loan you are given,
And you'll appreciate the life that you are livin'.
As a measure to see how well you are doing
Look to people who have practiced their 'wooing';
An example of success can be easily seen
If you closely examine a married team,
Who have spent their time in laughter and tears,
Especially those married fifty plus years!
The time has been well used and carefully planned,
Russell and Eleanor can proudly stand
And claim with pride, with heads held high,
(Or a bit or reluctance and a sigh),
That time well spent goes twice as fast
You know this when you look to the past.
And wonder where the time was spent,
You wonder where the years has 'went'.
But that was 'ago', you've still lots to give
So look to the future, and live, live, live!
We may not know what the future has stored,
But by using your loan well, you'll never be bored!
When the ultimate bell rings, let it loudly chime,
And claim to the world of your well used TIME.

Really!?

A picnic for family and friends,
Results in a multitude of tangled ends.
Each year, new ones appear,
While others just seem to disappear.
They gather at a waterfront home,
Green lawns to the shores do roam.
And clicks do form, of four or five
As they laugh and swim and dive.
There are those who gather at the food-
While others are in a gossip mood;
The children are a splendor to see them attack
With laughing, splashing and badminton match.
And a few new ones, an intellectual band,
Who don't know who's who in the gang,
Make observations with the company host,
Who is mild of manner and never boasts,
The stranger says," it's obvious, even though I'm new,
I can tell in just a moment or two,-
That these people are easily categorized.
Intellectually, and eventually by SIZE!.
And I can even do it by the way they dress,
Clothes make a person in a public nest.
That group is classified, as they eat from the platter,
As bulge's, fat, quite fat and fatter!
You can tell from their various suits, the age of the mass;
Their rolls are hiding their bathing suits enmasse'!
The other group is not quite as obese
They only use one hand to devour the feast.
And that group, with the gentleman not so smart,
The one with two hands of food, a belch and a fart
His talk is cheap and often vile,
He should be in an Out House pile.
Thanks for inviting me, it's been an interesting time.
But if I come again, let's go elsewhere to dine,
Because I have a question, and I am just assumin',
Are you sure these people are really HUMAN?"

SPEED

My job is one involving a smile and swiftness,
Serving mankind with surety and deftness.
My movements are fast and assured,
I've kept my body prepared as I matured.
But there are times when speed can be bizarre,
Especially when on ninety five north in a car.

FOUR SCORE AND FOUR

Four score and four years ago
My mother brought forth on this continent
A new Son, conceived on her wedding night,
And miraculously born five months later!
Claiming me as a miracle baby;
Accelerated in growth and maturity;
Her second child, Brucey, took longer.
Seven and a half months! (premature)
All the rest took nine months.
From which she coined the phrase.
'The first one comes anytime,
All the rest take nine months'.

The Under Takers

Carefully they bent,
Carefully they kneeled;
They could tell by looking,
That they were dead.

Gentleness was not in order now;
Delicate maneuvers unnecessary.
They wouldn't know the difference,
They were dead.

Some were undesirable,
Sucking the life from others;
Depriving them of living substances
Contributing to their deaths.

Vindictive action towards them!
Ruthless slaughter . . . .
Drag the life suckers out!
Toss them with the dead.

The battle is constant,
The attack is endless;
Only the strong will survive,
Let others meet their doom.

Then, a review of what remains,
Standing valiantly and strong,
Youthful resplendent beauty,
And free of those damn weeds!

Was He, Or Wasn't He?

She expectantly entered,
  Just a trifle haughty, but an impeccable arranger;
As she stepped into the Sanctuary,
  She froze- Her place occupied by a stranger!

Retreating to the rear pew in anger and disbelief,
  She fumed! That was her space!
She didn't sing. She didn't hear the sermon of relief;
  Bitterness extruded; There was a vendetta in place.

Who was this demented, despicable, intruder arrogant?
  Who forced her to a back row seat!
Who dared to occupy her seat so prominent
  Dressed so shabbily, not very neat?

He rose to speak and share, with a face of tears
  But she heard not the message given;
Within herself she broiled a campaign smear,
  He'd wish he could give up livin'.

While others gathered to say hello,
  She steamed and raced outside,
Then to coffee down below
  Readying her remarks so snide.

When her best friend spoke and asked why such disdain?
  Why she hadn't shook the hand that greeted us
He disappeared as he announced his claim,
  Saying that he was really our Savior Jesus!

Media Emulation

The loss of 'to' and 'you'
From English and 'American',
Replaced by 'Tuh' and 'Yuh'
Make it difficult to understand.
Done by the Media and a lazy few
Dims my listening to you.

Replacing the "A" for "O",
Pronounced "uh" and Oh",
Is causing me distress
Especially when the Media does it best!

To spread misuse that way,
Thus society responds to say,
"I went 'ta' see 'ya',
Or, "Glad ta meat 'cha'!

Instead it's slang they use,
Lazy speaking does ensue.
Then there's a change of 'er' for 'ur',
And let's not forget 'or' for 'er'.

So, Ah went ta git yuh, see,
Ta go fer uh walk wid me-
'Er' versus 'ur'
'Or' versus 'er'.
Is it Harford, Hartford or Hartferd?
Mispronunciation is absurd!

Then there's the loss of 'h', and sometimes 't'
So subtle, and the 'th' becomes a 'd', you see.
Now the 'th' changes once again,
We stretch the language with no pain.

So dey wen ta git ya, see,
Ta go fer uh walk wid me.
Doesn't that sound most charming?
It is also most alarming!

'Ta" for "to"
"Ya" for "you",
Has it changed your view?
Now it's really up to you!

The Accident

There is blood on the floor
Said the woman at the door
As she viewed the accident scene.

She stepped in to see
Tripped, skinned her knee
And how she did scream.

Her voice drew them around
As she lay on the ground
Gazing at the bloody stream.

The sight of which did sicken
And several were then stricken
They grasped something upon which to lean.

How the crowd then grew
And blocked the pending rescue
Then saw the ones getting green.

Quickly they ambled away
And spewed into the quiet bay
Thus polluting the water clean.

The Gift, Tied with a Blue Ribbon

He admired the scarf, so elegant,
But decided the cost too extravagant.
She contrarily said with reserve,
Buy it, it's something you deserve.
But alas and alack
He made a fast track
To a different part of the store,
To continue their mini shopping tour.
Two days later a package arrived,
Opening it he was very surprised,
Neatly wrapped with ribbon blue,
And a note that said, "Something for you"!
He pulled the ribbon to undo the bow,
Folded the ribbon carefully to stow,
And removed the scarf from the box
Thinking she was a lovely sly fox.
This wasn't the only occurrence of surprises from her,
By many blue ribbon bowed gifts his heart did stir.
Each he carefully pulled the blue ribbon bow,
Hanging them together all in a row.
This day he called on her to take her to dine,
She said she'd shower, and in a very short time,
She appeared coifuered, in blouse and skirt
Radiantly shining in her eyes a mischievous flirt.
But what amazed him most of the brilliant glow,
Tied around her blouse was a Blue Ribbon Bow!
She looked so ravishing, shining and clean,
His mind was flushed, what does it mean?
And he never saw her again is the story,
She's still standing there in all her glory.
And wondering why he didn't get the clue,
Of the Blue Ribbon Bow so easy to undo!

ONE TINY CELL: THE LIFE SAVER

What happened at the top of Reichenbach Falls,
It's really not impressive, no, not at all!
A silly argument basically about whose IQ is higher,
When it should have been about who's the better flyer.
We care not if it's relevant or profound,
Nor if they prayed on their way down,
No, more important is an unknown fact,
That Holmes' life was saved by an infinitesimal crack!
Oh sure, he claims he grabbed a branch
As through the air he did advance,
And it firmly held his muscular frame
While Moriarty continued to his heavenly plain?
In physics a body accelerates at 32' per second
Or is that 32' per second per second?
I know I wouldn't think that if I fell,
But it caused me to think of one little cell,
And the role it played in saving a life,
Of a person who fought against evil strife.
Yes, a little cell held fast and true
In a miniscule crack out of view.
With other cells they experienced that shock,
Hidden, where they forced themselves into solid rock!
And with all that added accelerating weight
They were the anchor to a great man's fate.
So Holmes, give thanks and loudly declare,
That your life was saved by a tiny root-hair.

Recollections

The Gauntlet

But mine arms be stained and bloody,
Sayeth his battle weary scarred up buddy;
How makest thou such delicate moves,
With arms whence ne'er scarred with grooves.
Quaffs thou on some magic draughts,
That protecteth thou from what others wrought?
Tellest thou me, oh scar-less Sire.
Can'st thou pull free of a rabbit's briar,
And nary once hast thou a drop pulsed forth,
How dost thee pluck without red froth?
A flower blossom protected with entwined barb,
That ordinary man be caused to shriek and sob?
What sayest thou? Who use-eth a sword so dauntless!
Thou protecteth me? Givest me your battle gauntlets?
Pithy, let me thankest ye ere I forget arms once red,
Knowest now mine arms no longer evidence that I bled!
How couldest I ne'er thinketh so; rare, hallow, love, empathy;
As grandfather's goatskin, cowhide, Bear Wallow Glove Company!

Lafayette Street

Busily they scurried along the shop-lined street,
But not too rushed to wave or nod to shoppers they'd meet.
Friendly the atmosphere of the passers-by
A congenial aura of helpfulness illuminated the sky.
Tisko's Market, with its ground coffee smell,
Near where Emma's fruit stand does dwell.
These memories return when certain aromas arise,
Of the long street with enticing shops on each side;
My youth returns, I'm elated to recall,
LaFayette street with its many stalls.
I walked its length to the North Elementary,
For an education that was rudimentary.
Also to Junior High, then on to Central High,
With its innumerable activities to keep one spry!
The street was alive with musical tones,
Enticing me to string along with my violin groans!
Even tried to imitate Benny Goodman and his clarinet,
Which caused the dogs to howl in the near-by vets!
Fascinating was the yearly arrival of the Gypsy group,
Who'd park in lots and occupy store front stoops.
Where their waste work was by incinerators destroyed
So the street was clean, no decaying so others were annoyed.
But then came the invasion and turned things around
Grove Street and LaFayette echoed with a new sound;
Language barriers soon were invariably instituted!
And new looks, shops closed, living there was unsuited!
But there is a laughingly recall of the old clarinet
And the smells and friendliness of the street LaFayette!

The Hammock

At 17 and a few days,
Two years of high school
And a year of farmers pay,
He was off to the boot camp pool.

"Strip out 'er garments there,
Pack 'em in uh box ta send,
You needn't keep yer unda'ware
Just change 'em when ya ken."

4 sets of skivies, white;
4 pair of socks, black;
2 pair of dungarees, too tight!
2 pair of shoes the socks to match.

"Yore suitcase you won't need fur clothes,
Now yore gornna pack a Sea-bag,
But first everything' must be rolled,
Yore hammock, mattress, with uh tag."

Stencils issued with your name,
Indelible ink, on each article fine,
All the colors were the same,
Clothes stops? For the hanging on the line.
(While yore at it, keep this in mind
No 'Orange Pennants' do I wanna find!

"This is how you do it, watch closely me lad-dees,
Roll yore clothes, then they'll be wrinkle free,
Fold yore hammock an mattress into three's
Place the Sea-Bag in the middle, see?"

With that, he folded up the ends,
Around the Sea-Bag, end to end
The ropes he twisted once, 'en then
Around the Sea-Bag, knotted at the bend.

"As ya ken see, a place for everything,
Everything in it's place.
Nothing lost, no, not a thing,
Ready now, no loss of space.

"But why the hammock and mattress thin?"
Some one dared to question him.
He looked and smiled a smile waxing,
"No bunks on ships, they's only stanchion swings."

What? No bunks or beds on which to stay?
"Should you to these ships be assigned,
 They'll toss 'en turn, 'en pitch and sway
You'll be thankful for this hammock fine.

With each toss and turn the ship you see,
The bunk could make you sea-sick,
The hammock responds to gravity
So to the head you'll not run so quick."

These thoughts returned for years
As he packed his hammock beige;
Till he left it home while on liberty,
New ships had no hooks for a hammock's sway.

They were the last to receive this bed so dear,
An era gone, all gone I suspect,
No longer a place to 'stow yore gear'
No longer need to 'clear the decks'.

But the memory remains;, he was one of the few,
Who shouldered his gear of the same weight as him,
And brought them home for years to use,
This hammock now tied between two limbs.

Church Flowers

Uh guy an' uh gal, fun lovin' pals,
Spent uh happy lifetime ta-gether;
They decided early on, of helpin' they were fond,
An' decorating church steps wuz uh treasur'.
Til' wid uh cane they walked,
 though the distance wuz short,
Thuh carryin' flowahs there caused displeasur'.
So with increased limp,
 to give someone uh hint,
They enlisted uh passa'-by of masculin' genda'.
Sympathetic to their need,
he responds to their deed,
Gave as much help as he could renda'.
But then came uh bit,
the plants they did tip,
There-by disturbin' the graphic splenda,.
No, this way not that,
she said without tact,
As to her directions he did surrenda'.
Now the moral of this,
is that they still live in bliss,
But the passa'-by wonders, should he bill her?
10-10-10- dan

Cabbage in Refrigerator

'Cabbage in refrigerator', said the sign,
    A reminder to the serving team.
"There are buns to slice, and tomatoes too,
    And where did you put the whipping cream?"
Jocularly but firmly, the banter went on
    While some men set the chairs in place;
And the table cloths, and knives and forks,
    Napkins, but without a China plate!
Back in the kitchen the banter continued
    With much laughter and lilting sparks;
The cheese was spread; the ham was rolled,
    "But the turkey's too thin", 'twas one remark!
      (Cakes were sliced and beans heated
        They were the kind that never repeated)
Bar-B-Que. beef placed in two pots
    And the flame turned up to high,
And coffee was readied quite soon,
    One sip and an exclamatory sigh—-
"Did anyone put grounds in the basket?"
    Was a questioned look of surprise!
"It's not weak, you use too much milk"
    Someone quickly claimed in reprise.
Who are these people who work with so young a heart,
    Whose ages belie their nimble minds?
Who in service to others have dedicated lives
    Learned in a period from the beginning of time?
Some so short the lower shelves can't be reached
    Or are unable to reach the bottom of the sink;
Some more nimble, some a little less,
    Some can do it before you can wink or blink!
Efficiency reins as they put out the eggs,
    In a manner so devilishly swift;
With pickles and olives and gherkins too
    All placed artistically in a serving dish—-

Then all was ready, after the floor was mopped,
   It was resting time for the bunch,
Before the onslaught and the arrival
   Of those who'd partake in the lunch.
What, you ask, are the names of this crew
   With such a devotion to all humanity?
Why the answer is simple, this their reply
   "We're in the Good Book under anonymity"
But just from memory, to mention a few
   There were four BOBS and a BOBBIE RAY
A JENNETTE, a MARGARET, a CATHY, a SHIRLEY,
   And MARTHA who really didn't stay!
      {I think she had to wash someone's feet
         Or burden herself with another service feat}
All this done in service as in a response
   To others in their hour of need—-
'Twas a funeral luncheon they had prepared,
   Just 'uh plantin' God's mustard seed.
In all the hustle-bustle and aftermath there
   Is one simple indicator!
'Twas a sign on the floor that simply read,
   'Cabbage in refrigerator'.

Tire Swing

The tire swing is idle, just hanging there,
    No tracks, no scuffing or swaying at all.
The day is calm, no movement of air,
    At the tire swing near the snow dusted wall.

It is a symbol of joy and laughter
    And squeals of sudden delight,
As young ones reach toward the rafters
    Experiencing a wild bird in flight.

'Push again' is their melodious clamor
    As though they will reach the sky,
And they exhilaratingly giggle and stammer
    Attaining a jubilant high.

'You look so small down there'
    Is the youthful high pitched cry,
And they swing without fear or care
    As they pretend that they do fly.

Such stories could be boastfully told,
    By the swing at the snow dusted wall;
Of moments more precious than gold,
    If the now silent swing could recall.

You Can Tell At A Glance

There was a time when young girls
Imitated their elders, even copying their curls.
Manners were learned and daily practiced,
'You'll never know to whom you're attracted'.
They wore their shawls, gloves and hats,
They stood tall, never slouched, not that.
Yes, and please, thank you ever so much,
Polite phrases learned with a smiling touch.
May I help you? To an elder's delight,
'After you', said with a curtsey slight.
Dresses buttoned to their neck at least,
No luring for some leering beast.
Manners were then always a pride,
Ladies walked, chin up, a gliding stride.
Yes, remember then when ladies wore bonnets,
And to ladies, some men even sang sonnets.
Men recognized a lady on sight,
Would never ogle or degrade or slight.
Now I seldom see the courageous few,
But I still tip my hat, is one of them you?

The Old Swing Is Gone

As one looks at the snow covered wall
Where a tree once stood so strong and tall,
Under drifts there, out of sight,
Is the wall that witnessed children's delight.
The morning Sun casts shadows long and slight,
All pointing, in black and white, to that location site,
But it's not there, the wall is lonely, the tree is gone.
The silence is eerie, then broken by birds of song,
Looking for a landing perch, and foods of any array.
Where once the tree served as a place to stay
Now they swoop upward in utter dismay!
Circle and choose a site of lesser appeal.
But this tree knows not the joyous squeals,
Only that of harsh howling winds and breeze.
And the wall encased by the crusty freeze
Reflects on the sounds once caused by the swing,
And feels the dismay of those on the wing.
As the raucousness now continues to ring,
In adjustment to the destruction of the swing.

The Indian Head

Eight inches beneath the ground
Is where an Indian head was found.
1874 is the date upon this cent,
Now it's a penny never to be spent.
Found by a landscaper named Jerry,
After going to work via the N.L ferry.
The coin into his pocket he saved
For posterity or perhaps a trade.
Till one day he discovered a collector man,
And he gave the coin to his Uncle Dan.

The Three C's

Decorative roof tops are seldom seen,
It makes one wonder, who engineered these scenes?
Out of sight, except for the sky,
The question arises, Why? Oh Why?
The answer in one of the 3-C's hoopla
Chimney's, clouds and of course Cupolas.
So attractive, so superbly built,
Though through the ages some slightly tilt.
And again we must take note,
In the past all the public saw was acrid smoke-
But now, there is beauty at which no one can stare,
So build a viewing platform and a set of stairs!
Roof tops and chimneys and cupolas too,
Climb up here and enjoy a great view!

Peggy and Friend

Peggy and friend at age nine, they say,
Decided on an adventure one bright sunny day,
To look for treasures and find out the truth,
Of what was buried near the old tree roots!
Carefully they approached the stone strewn place,
And began digging, to find even a trace,
Of what was supposedly hidden there
With every inch they would intensely stare!
To their amazement after only a foot,
They were startled as up they looked.
Standing there was an officer of the law,
Hands on hips and a square set jaw;
What are you doing in these burying grounds?
These are sacred Indian mounds!
Frightened they were taken away,
Their adventure interrupted, a permanent delay;
Innocent of wrong doing was the judge's claim,
Merely a childhood adventure for fame to gain.
Just an industrious imaginative foray,
Just intelligent young girls at inquisitive play!

Tributes

The Souk

Crowded into three meters square
   A kaleidoscope of cubical display,
Shoulder to shoulder no heads bared
   Language barriers soon decay.

There you see a woman veiled,
   The next one exposed of face,
Still internationalism prevailed,
   Good haggling sets the pace!

The aromas change as you do parade
   Amidst the raucous din,
'Come, come- look, look, make a trade'
   "Or buy this cruddy thing!"

'How much, how much', you do ask.
   You repeat yourself again and again.
'Cheap, I give good price,' is his rasp,
   But proudly you refrain.

'Only 400 dirham' is his plea
   You say 'no' to his startled look.
'How much you give, come see . . .'
   Inside a voice says, 'don't be took'.

Again in his candid voice exclaims,
   '400 dirham, cheap, what you pay?'
Your mind is racing to survive,
   '75 dirham' it does say.

You voice your opinion very clear,
   He looks depressed and aghast;
He grabs the wrapping paper near,
   '320 is all I ask!'.

No! The inner voice repeats
   You hear yourself say '75',
And your body follows your feet
   Heading back outside.

'250' sez the excited voice
   And his friend comes to his aid,
With another artifact of choice
   You're weakening and afraid!

Again you make your offer,
   He comes down a little lower,
You see he's getting softer,
   His voice a little slower-

'OK, one hundred I'll offer you'
   He then says 'one twenty's it!'
'No'. And to the door you continue;
   He almost has a fit.!

Finally he acquiesces to your skill,
   Dejectedly he wraps your gift,
And takes your paper bill;
   His look is sad, a little miffed.

You chuckle to yourself,
   And continue through the stalls,
You see your gift on another shelf,
   So in you go with gall!

To price this little item
   Is your intended task;
His eyes are twinkling gems
   'One hundred is all I ask'!

Do they have a wireless state
   That is connected to all the shops?
Are they trying to intimidate
   And see your face go flop??

OH there is no place you can go
   To buy spices or your fruit,
Where you feel so high, then low
   As when you parade on through a souk.

But it's a worthwhile experience,
   You'll be happy you did strive,
Don't worry if you lose a bit,
   You're really lucky to survive!
Agardir, Morac

Young Artists

I sit with crayons, pencils, chalk
Oblivious to the surrounding talk;
Concentrating on the task I've chosen
Life on paper forever frozen
With primitive, loving, thoughts portrayed.

Although I'm amateurish with my strokes
Imagination guides my sketching folks,
Freedom of thought and inner desires
Flows through my fingers to inspire
The primitive, loving, thoughts portrayed.

Gentle exchange of creative minds
Uninhibited with truth or oppressed by time,
Waxing with enlightened knowledge of years
Interpreted through mental eyes to visual ideas
The primitive, loving, thoughts portrayed.

My Mother

My mother was very young once,
A beauty, vivaciously alive and yet very staid.
She was athletic, she was agile, a jumper,
   Over five barrels while on skating blades!
She ran with carefree fleetness
   At local fair-ground tracks,
Win or lose, she looked ahead,
   And never once looked back.
What's done is done, leave it behind
   Always look ahead,
Somewhere in the distance
   Is a goal or the choice of being led.
Let nothing here deter you
   From your chosen way or life,
And should you err in judgment,
   Know YOU can conquer strife!
Those are some of the vibrant signals
   I received in my youth
She let these facts escape
   As ways to reminisce a truth.
Story after story she divulged
From time to time of course,
From when she was a youngster
   And used to ride a horse.
And how she and another sister
   Would practice their violins at best,
Depending on how they were seated,
   One you see was right handed, the other was left!

Tin Cans And Battleships

Tin Cans, the backbone of the Navy-
Few people know of its destructive abilities,
Nor of the men who served and of their bravery-
In making the ship one of evasive mobility

No task too large or too small,
Once started the ship plowed on through,
To their duty stations, they answered the call;
And below decks was the engineering crew!

The unknown men deep down inside,
With spotless engines and no oil rags strewn.
Who seldom saw the sun topside,
Kept generators and engines very well tuned.

These unsung heroes deep in the bowels
Answering the commands of whistles and bells,
Never knowing the reason why or see scowls
Or see the fury or their raising hell-

One man clearly recalls one battle night,
Feeling the vibrations throughout the boat,
Hearing the blasts not seeing the sight,
Throwing the levers, keep her afloat!

He sits there at a Veterans dinner
No one knows of his personal endeavors,
Each man there came home, a battle winner
But 17 times this man tended his levers.

Years from now will anyone recall,
Or where all these men have been?
Will their names be found upon a wall?
Especially one named Eugene.

Dr. "K" Where Are You?

Brilliant! An Avid reader of great books!
Sometimes two a day.
And he remembered what he read!
Not as clever as his younger brother
With a photographic mind,
But still clever, engaging,
Speaking on any subject entertainingly
And intellectually.
Now, he lays there in a semi-conscious state:
He recognizes me, but slips off in a doze.
Painfully he unconsciously scratches,
"Why am I here? What did I do wrong?"
Is his comment.
"So, did I fall? I'm cold, let's go to Florida,
  Let's go to Hawaii,
  Do I live here now?
  These nurses are great".
Or he refuses to get up;
  To wash,
  To eat,
  To walk,
But when he needs to get up
He struggles,
Without waiting for assistance.
When awake, he is cognizant
And entertaining, reasonably
Articulate, seldom complaining!
At the same time,
  Stubborn, non-complying
  And asking if one of the Nurses
  Would go to Florida with him,
Then, he forgets, and
It starts all over again.
No GOD would let this happen!
Not to a person who
Dedicated his life to helping others,

And influencing thousands.
He made a difference!
He helped create
  Doctors,
  Teachers,
  Lawyers,
  Nurses,
And an endless number of
Other worthwhile citizens.
Now he lays there—-
Metamorphosing and deteriorating!
NOT FAIR!
Sleep talk is cruel—-
"Gotta do something, Danny,
I can't live like this"!
"OH MY, OH MY"
As he relives the pain:
"Danny, can't you do something?"
And I am helpless . . .
Dr. "K", where are you?

I Trod

Neigh on to a hundred years ago, or so,
   I trod where horses trod,
And followed along lines so slim
   As though balancing on a rail most trim;
My arms held out to either side
   Hands extended shoulder high.
I walked, I ran, I skipped, bare feet of course,
   Till the lines curved at an intersection, lost!
Then turned around, dodged a wagon with a trotting horse,
   And followed its line as I had the first, without remorse,
With eyes so bright, reflecting the radiant sky,
   I found myself looking back somewhat shy,
And saw my footprints scarcely covering the track indentations
   Thus wondered if anyone would follow my prints without trepidations.
Those imbedded lines on that dirt road forever remained in my mind,
   It's been an example; it's been a clean clear sign,
Like a line of life, it's meant to me a saving grace:
   My foot prints must lead somewhere for a followers pace
Who might be seeking an example of excellence
   Or a way to quell some unexpected turbulence.
Now I look down the paved streets with a little sorrow,
   No, I don't miss the mud, or smells that linger till the morrow,
But I miss the free 'spiritness' that we all exhibited,
   The 'spontaneousness' that now seems prohibited.
Thus I wonder if anyone followed the trail I left behind,
   And who will leave the emulation trail for the next in line?
Ah, the memories—nigh on to a hundred years, or so,
   I walked that track left by the wheel,
With extended arms and hands to feel
   The need of others who lost their way back
And set them upright on the slim old track—
   I nursed them,
   I loved them,
   I listened with attentive ear,
   And helped wipe away many a tear;

Always in my mind's eye I saw that radiant day of yore,
   With the happy faces as they glanced upon the smile I wore.
So as I balanced on life's trackless line for miles
   Found more healing results when treated with wholesome smiles.
And I should know,
I've done it neigh on to a hundred years, or so,
   Since I trod where horses trod,
     No, not alone, I had God.

The Empty Desk and Vacant Chair

The desk is empty and a void permeated the air
The radio is silent as is the vacant chair;
I keep listening for a lusty voice to drone,
And sharply command 'answer that phone'!
The jar of candy kisses last longer than before
I'd rather be filling it just a little more;
Occasionally I am awakened from a solemn nell
And I listen intently for the sound of 'THE BELL',
But it doesn't chime as it once did in boast,
"Hey, hear that?" loudly claimed the host.
The smell of soup, or sandwich grand,
The exclamation of 'that's good, man-o-man!'
Twill be this way for a long long while
But I'll look at the desk, remember and smile,
And maybe go and play a game of solitaire
To see how well I'll be able to compare—
Now, I sit here a stranger amongst strangers, yet a friend
The day is unseasonably warm as all into this mass try to blend.
The empty desk is alone like a blossoming forsythia in December
Unusual, but the once brilliant beauty is still remembered.
Who now will be the innovator of interesting phrases
Call attention to passing beauty in various stages—
Choice descriptive terms so elegantly and poignantly presented
Made one sigh and moan as he spoke and lamented;
And then I choked with an agonizing start
When they sang 'How Great Thou Art'.
And my vision clouded and in lonely despair,
Seeing the empty desk and vacant chair . . .

Gretel (Marilynn?)

She had dark attractive hair,
    Dark brown eyes alive and merry
An oval face so clean and fair
    And her lips the hue of a cherry.
Face to face we stood in a nervous wait
    For instructions on how to act;
She stepped right and left
    in a stiffed-legged gait
Then stopped with fingers
    hooked behind her back
They forced me to dance with her,
    As her partner we stepped and swirled
What she thought of me I never heard,
    But to me she was a GIRL!
I was the boy eager to please
    But unschooled in the refinement of the society bit!
She was the girl I would like to squeeze
    But didn't know why or how to accomplish it.
Finally we were given a musical command:
    Right foot first, left foot then
Round-about and back again.
    "My you did that very well
Who could all this sake foretell
    Right foot first, left foot then
Round-about and back again!"
The memories come flooding back.
    So real and so alive!
This happened years ago,
    Before the class of forty-five-
Its stayed with me during the years,
    Still ringing in my ears,
Of a vision on stage of a dance
    That still puts me in a trance,

That girl with dark attractive hair,
    Dark brown eyes alive and merry,
An oval face so clean and fair,
    And lips with the hue of a cherry.
It was right foot first, and left foot then
    Round about and back again,
"My you did that very well
    Who could all this sake foretell
Right foot first, left foot then
    Round about and back again . . ."

Real Dedication & Lack Of It

(True Life Results)

He was ten and a menace,
He was a terror to his parents;
He hated school, it was a penance,
That he was L.D. was quite apparent.

Fourth grade and couldn't read,
The result of 'No child left behind'.
Education's answer to his social need;
Push him ahead, don't be unkind.

So it was till he met one teacher real,
Whose quiet demeanor and concern,
Who looked into the boy, awakened the zeal,
Attracted the boy, so he desired to learn!

The struggle was there, but he now was inspired;
He looked forward to every tomorrow,
Excitedly he developed, no longer tired,
Weekends with no school were a time of sorrow.

His parents were enthralled by all this,
When by springtime he could read!
His life had changed, no longer a risk,
They could smile and finally breathe.

Who was this teacher so prepared, so superb?
That caused such a dramatic change,
Who so influenced a boy once disturbed,
Enabling the reading of books of wide range?

Ecstasy at home now quietly reined,
His life no longer of a silenced mute;
But a jubilant, radiant kind of game,
Reading was now a basic root.

From a reading skill of naught,
He surpassed the struggling mass;
Able now to create deep thought,
He no longer gave people sass.

This brought his parents to school,
The meeting so jovial and proud,
With tears they praised the rule,
Next year he'd be back if allowed.
Next year devastation was the result
His beloved teacher had retired,
His behavior soon became an insult,
The new teacher was not inspired.

Try as they might, it was a miserable mess,
He reverted to abusive actions, they say,
His demeanor denied any chance of success,
A bright future had now turned to gray.

A capable mind no longer alert,
A capable mind no longer can read,
A capable mind that once did search,
Now left, no one nourished the seed.

Who failed to respond to this child?
Who allowed him to forge ahead?
Who left him to revert to the wild?
Educators who are dead in the head!

Egypt

We're trudging, we're trudging
    all over the land
On the right and the left of us
    we only see sand.
We don't use sun lotion
    because we do think
That it increased thirst
    when there's nothing to drink.

Chorus:
Away, away with sun and RUNS
With sun and runs, with sun and runs
Away, away with sun and runs
The song of the Egyptian traveler.

We never eat strange food
    because of the grease
And one little bite
    sends one to the round seat
Can you imagine a more horrible sight
Than yourself in such agony
    in the dark of the night?

Chorus:

We never drink water
    that sits in the sun
For one little sip
    causes the stomach to run
Can you imagine a sorrier mess
Than finding a place
    when in such distress?

Chorus:

Ma Sar Oud is coming
    our leader today
He'll guide us to shops
    where we don't have to pay
He leads us to temples
    while in the hot sun
Why do we do this,
    is it for fun?

Chorus:

Go to the temple
    of the great Aga "Kan"
Ignore the hot wind
    that blows 'ore the sand
But he doesn't climb
    the sand blasted way
He sits and relaxes
    in the cool of the shade.

Chorus:

They say that they like us
    they say we're alright
So why do they wake us
    in the dark of the night?
We walk and we run
    and sometimes we crawl
To taxies, to buses,
    and carriages small.

Chorus:

Tomorrow sez he
    or right now is the time
I show you the secrets
    of temples sublime

Of kings with six hats
    and some really odd ways
And priest who wash statues
    three time a day.

Chorus:

So I sit on the deck
    real late at night
And gaze at the river banks
    and twinkling light
Its time to reflect on
    what Ma Sar Oud said
But my brain doesn't function
    I think its gone dead.

Chorus:

"Ha Urh Us" not Horus
    is that what he said?
Is he the one
    that wears a girls head?
Or is he the father
    of the Queen of the Nile?
This stuff is confusing
    after awhile.

Chorus:

Just eat a little
    Of all the food piled
That's really not meat loaf
    but Nile crocodile
Whether its green
    or whether it's white
If it' not safe
    you'll find out tonight.

Chorus

We're walking, we're talking
    along their dirt streets
With its smells and sounds
    of Bah-Shee, Bah-shee
In this land of theirs
    they hold so dear
How many children
    will live till next year?

Chorus:

Look backward, look backward
    a difficult feat
To re-experience
    the sand and the heat
And the primitive needs
    of the children we saw
It's hard to do in
    this comfort galore.

Chorus

And so our adventure
    has come to an end
We arrived meeting strangers
    that soon became friends
From this strange land
    with its ancient past
We hope that these friendships
    forever will last.

Secrets Shared

Secrets shared forever, never to be revealed,
Faithful in all endeavors, love eternally sealed.
Bosom buddies till the end of time,
Companions, trusted thoughts divine;
Our devotion, happy memories that remain,
I'll cherish them without any moment of disdain.
Bravely faced the crushing news,
That soon from earth you'd make the move;
This deterred you not, showed little strife,
Within you dwelt that cherished light.
Strength and Joy with you I found,
Your melodious voice, oh what a sound!
Now you've chosen to leave me alone,
I'll survive, but remember when I'm grown.
When a child loses a parent, the past is lost;
When a parent loses a child, a future the cost!
Now with memories of you I'll keep busy,
We love you more than life, brave and courageous Izzy.
She left us
At the Solstice;
The alignment of
Heavenly bodies cast a
Shadow of majestic splendor
To accompany her on her heavenly journey.
Now, with each Solstice we'll remember,
As we look to the Universe,
For that new shining star.
And the Astronomers
Will call that new
Heavenly body,
IZZY of the
WINTER
SOLSTICE.

Doctor's Care

I came to you in some agony
And listless for life's great stand;
You looked at me with courage
And then carefully took my hand.
You spoke with me through
Your eyes and your voice
And I felt the bond, you'd make the correct choice-
Far from home, a little insecure,
You said relax, make mine yours.
How loudly and sincere
Your eyes did speak!
From them I knew I had
Trusting souls of peace;
And intellect, trained in
Science, Love and Art.
No room in there for hate,
Or fear, or societal larks.
Deep, probing introspect
And guidance from beyond
With whom you have connected
And feel that guiding arm,
Transferring that deep unconsciousness
Into cognizant understanding,
To which each transmitting axon
Responds to your eyes commanding.

A Saint

No matter how little she had, she found enough to give to someone else.
No matter what the need, she found time to serve and comfort-
Loyal, helpful service, from a school long since forgotten,
She was tutored in these ways!
The women received nothing,
   She was so self-reliant!
   She was always busy attending to others,
   She was always grateful for friends,
   She was always a lady in my eyes.
   She had a faith that transcends and encompassed all major beliefs-
One that claimed Natural Goodness as the sustenance for the soul.
   It drew on energies of beauty,
   It drew on energies of love,
   It drew on energies of respect,
   It drew on energies of discipline,
   It drew on energies of friends.
Like a birch laden with ice in a storm,
She bent, carried the load, and knelt to touch the ground,
But with the help of wind and sun, shook off the ice and cold and,
Resumed her up-right stance, and continued to grow into maturity-
With gentle understanding, compassion and spirit of goodness.
A haven for those in need, like the juniper tree is to birds Offering shelter in storms,
Offering shade in the heat,
Offering protection from attacks.
Like a tree giving life,
Spreading her arms so as to receive all those seeking refuge.
Her reward was:
    Seeing pleasure in their eyes,
    Seeing relief in their eyes,
    Seeing a belief in their eyes,
    Seeing thankfulness in their eyes.
Still, she sometimes felt alone;
   Looking for that mental contact, not physical, but mental,
   Looking for that psychological commitment,
   Looking for that aesthetic touch and engulfment,
   Looking for that cloak, that calmness,

That comes when comforted by deep understanding and trust and love-
    The Agape` love at which one arrives
    When thoughts merge and blend into
    An astonishing wonderment of revelation.
Good music, good conversation, good friends,
And a belief that all who knew her, loved her,
For her kindness and concern-
They loved her because of many things, and will
Remember her because she was
Loving, virtuous, faithful and KIND.
A good mother and a good friend.

He Was Seventeen

He was seventeen.
His father said,
  Don't tell your mother
  She would never forgive me.
He passed the physical two days later.
So proud, he left with a small satchel,
  It contained a change of underwear
  And sandwiches for the overnight trip.
Training was arduous for his group,
But for him it was a blast!
A choice of duty, because he was bright,
Of course, he knew, a gunner in flight!
  And a radioman, at code he was best;
  He practiced both, no need for rest.
Then came the moment of flight to his ship
That spot down there, just a mere slip!
Then refueling and wait for the time,
Anxiety built, then the command to fly.
  Into his compartment, no hesitance,
  No thought of the morrow.
The engine roared, a surge on the belts,
And off the deck, an Avenger to be.
  Bombs away, torpedoes away, the flack
  Was thick, It shattered plexi-glass;
  They climbed up high after the pass.
Divers Zeroed in, they fought tooth and nail,
They survived that attack, and on the way back,
  An Armada was seen,
  The pilot said, if we radio now,
  We may be all dead.
We've go to tell, the radioman claimed,
  Besides, we've got ammo,
  We'll survive.

So the radioman struck the key in
Dots and dashes;
   At the mother ship,
   Planes immediately dispatched
   To the zone of terror.
Another attack, They Zeroed in!
Stinger and turret blazed away;
   But it didn't matter
   Reliefs on the way.
Hook down, flaps at full,
A tattered Avenger landed at last'
The pilot climbed down
   They opened the rear
   But he didn't respond
'How old was he?'
They asked of the scene:
Today he was Seventeen.

I first read about this incident in the 1940's.
Having flown in an Avenger, I was able to
recall the episode and felt I had to write about
it. I wonder how the father felt . . .

An Unknown Hero

Inspired by Ed Carroll

I made the jump!
Free fall, then the jounce,
The bounce, the swinging
And the sway—
   Into the unknown
   Into the darkness
   Into the area of the uninvited!
Then the jar, and the pain and benevolent darkness!
I awoke to splints on my arm,
I awoke to pain in my leg and back,
I awoke to the entire right side throbbing.
Then the confinement and healing,
In a prison.
After six months, release—-
They sent me home.
Almost sixty years ago-
Young and indestructible,
I recovered and made my way overlooking
The infirmities—
Now, with cane and hobble
I make my way, but;
   I keep the smile.
   I keep the cheer.
   I am alive,
   While many comrades sleep!
Through the years of pain and misery,
I was happy and had no regrets-
Yes, I made the jump
   For the unknown
   For my loved ones
   For my country
   For those who thoughtlessly shout,
     Anti American slogans!

From them I'd like a thank you,
From the rest,
I did it for you!
Yes, I made the jump
And thank you for the privilege
To have served.

Quite A Guy

If ya hear uh person moan,
'En they say "I hurt ma bone",
Send 'um ta Doctor Gaccione.

If their hand is achin' bad
'En theys really very sad,
Send 'em ta Doctor Gaccione.

If their shoulder's not uh workin'
'En the pain now is uh worsen',
Send 'em ta Doctor Gaccione.

Afta operatin' theys stitched
Wrap 'em up all fixed
Courtesy uv Doctor Gaccione.

Then they'll sing in aria tones
When they ken use their achin' bones,
Thanks to Doctor Daniel Gaccione!
  (even though they couldn't sing before)

DEVASTATION

Devastation! That's my feeling at this moment. It's raining and I hear the thunder rolling, a low growling then an occasional sharp snap and again the low rolling grumble. It fits my mood. Ordinarily I find this stimulating and uplifting, but not today. Recent news has caused irritation and resentment and some anger. Also adding to my depression was my witnessing a bedraggled, unkempt, slovenly looking, urchin-like person, a burden on society, an embarrassment to mankind. What kind of justice allows life to continue in this manner and remove a life of kindness, love, industry and adoration? Joyfulness has been removed. The separation is supposedly only temporary: even that knowledge isn't satisfying. Glory, love, honor, an uplifting spirit, concern, respect, a forgiving heart, intelligence, all gone in one fleeting moment of quietness. It was a rather long time in coming, a needless period spent in preparation for that one quiet moment. Everyone knew the inevitable but were they really prepared? In my case it was one of my few moments of depending upon the miracle of hope: not realistic, that word, hope! It sort of intones an unattainable idea that someone will come forth and save the world. J.C. supposedly did that 2000 years ago and still hasn't succeeded. Justice? I guess I'm really a little bitter about this loss to mankind at least 30 years before its time. There is no compensation for such a loss to your family, and, especially ours. I have sat for over an hour trying to put my feeling into words. We all know we will be the victims of death eventually and we sort of lie to ourselves about being prepared, but we never really are. I knew Joyce would not survive long and I had sort of resigned myself to this end, but the empty, useless, devastating feeling of remorse and regret whelms up inside when the moment of truth is known, and you realize how totally insignificant you are in trying to comfort someone, or remove that knot in your abdomen. I have only good memories of Joyce. If we comforted her in any way, I'm glad.

O sinister scepter of insincere deceptiveness
Lurking ominously for a choice of innocence
Who controls your orneriness of intent?
For your mistakes, to whom do you repent?

Be gone. There are many that deserve your visit,
Why do you choose a magnificent embodiment of humanity?
Be Gone. There are many that desire your visit.
Serve those indulgent, miscreants of calamity;

Touch those who serve not the minds with love and compassion
Touch those who leach away the energy of good willed congregations
Touch those who take advantage and pursue selfish incantations

Heaven Ought To Be

I'm waiting here to travel on,
   I'm gonna climb to the mountain top.
When I get there,
   I'll see the place where
     Heaven ought to be
   I'll see the place where
     Heaven ought to be—
It's waiting there
Like I'm waiting here
I'll climb and take a look
   And I'll see the place where
     Heaven ought to be
It's waiting there for me—
But I'm not ready
   To make that trip,
This mountain peak is firm
   And sound
So I'll linger here
   On solid ground
There are many more
   That I must help;
Can't just stand around
   By my self—
Yet the time will come
   When I can't climb any more
But if I've seen that place
   Where heaven should be
Then I've accomplished a goal
   Without keeping score
Of the good I've done
   For the souls asea,
And I've seen the place
   Where heaven ought to be.

Though the mountain's high
   And I ache and ache
I'll climb up there to view the place
   Where heaven ought to be.

And When I'm down
   I'll remember the sight
Continuing my drive
   To do the right;
The day will come
   When they come for me
And lay my ashes
   Near by the sea
But until that time,
   I'll climb and climb
For that view to challenge me,
   And lift my spirits to a new high
   Maintaining my hopes and visions strong
   Instilling in me a lifetime song,
'Climb that peak so I can see,
The place where heaven ought to be'.

SOLITUDE

Solitude, a time to be alone
Yet a time to be united
With ones thoughts—
Solitude, the relief from oppression
Yet a time to delve into ones inner self,
For freedom—-
Solitude, that period when you are
Influenced by nature to stimulate
Good ideas and well being.
Solitude, the reaching deep within
For release from reality,
To the secret garden of beauty
Where wishes and hope reside.
Break down those barriers
That confine compassion and love,
Let them flood and pulsate
Through ones being,
Emitting an aura that encompasses
Those who are faint of heart;
Strengthening the resentful with courage
To be forgiving
And accepting their limitations:
   Be the influence for emulation,
   Be the spirit of freedom,
   Be the source of knowledge.
Break down your barriers
And let yourself run free.
 Solitude ...
    Solitude.

Springtime

I only see Springtime
   When I walk with you,
I only see Summer
   When I look at a view,
No matter if Winter
   Is stormy or dark,
You instilled your springtime
   Deep in my heart;
I walk without shoes
   On paths that are clear,
Even in darkness
   There is nothing to fear–
I only see Springtime
   When you hold my hand,
I only see summer
   All over the land.
It's your "springtime"
   View on everything dear,
No matter if freezing
   There is Summertime near.
Without your goodness
   I walk with despair,
You perfect the imperfect
   So it shines, unaware,
That your opulence now,
   Illuminates your soul,
Making it springtime,
   Removing the cold.
So I only see springtime
   When I walk with you,
I only see summer
   Believing in you!

In a Dark Wood

for Eugene

In a Dark Wood walks a man for all ages, past and present-
Upon his face there beams a hint of a smile,
   which radiates and outlines the path-
This Dark Wood is traveled by many
   in a declining twilight.
Some travel on in darkness, groping
   for a way to trod:
But the illumination from the inner glow of
   this man lightens the way for him,
This inner glow was kindled there within
   years ago
And was continually fanned and fueled
   through love of mankind
   through respect for all
   through concern for the welfare of others,
   in the drying of a tear,
   in rising above petty qualms,
      entering into the arena of discord
      he stayed the charging hordes—-
One man unafraid to speak,
One man with a trusting, listening ear,
One man whose hand,
   whether on a tiller
   whether on a shovel
   whether on a brush
   whether holding a pen
   or even a weed,
   or quahaug tongs
Never too busy to lend that hand
   to a justifiable cause.

Were you to meet this man, there was
   always a genuineness
   always an intensity
   always a smile
     that said,
  I'm glad to see you.
And when you left, you left with a faint spark
   or afterglow that you could use, if you desired,
     to start the conflagration
     so as to illuminate your way
     and incite glory in those you encountered.
So it will be in that Dark Wood
   where many will travel—
His infectious inner glow
   will brighten the way
   for those less able
And when my time comes to travel there,
I hope the spark that I received
   from him will enable me to lead others through-
And they will say . . .
In a Dark Wood walks a man for all ages
   past and present.

A Certain Kind Of Freedom

for Truus

There's a certain kind of Freedom
That comes to every life;
It's a Freedom that one attains
When relieved of cruel strife!
The love is there, locked deep inside
But the truth still remains,
Of the torturous moments past
And feelings of disdain.
This, created by the obligation of serving and doing right-
Only to experience threats,
From a mind no longer bright.
It is not due to conscious degrading acts,
The mind is ill, no longer capable
Of quelling these attacks.
It's full of fear, it's full of questions,
And other dark items one wants to mention.
It doesn't understand the lack of control
It doesn't recognize the one it loved to hold!
Now, the illness encourages disorientation and abuse,
Fear replaces adoration, a sorry truth-
The psyche chains the wandering mind, imagining;
No control over wobbling limbs, the walk now kinda' staggering-
Now, all that's far behind.
No sleepless nights, worries over creaking floors,
A burden lifted, now a little sunshine
In the knowledge he's safe behind solid doors,
Where trained techs calm his unsure ways,
Administers, to keep him happy, in his final days.
Now the Freedom, and time to heal,
Now the inner emotions one can feel.
The time will come when memories are of joyous times
And One is free to recall and even relive moments fine.
The time has come, I did my best,
Freedom's here, I passed the test.

Did Anybody Know?

Discontent, disheartened, a dismal beginning of a snowy day;
Life had been cruel, life no longer had any interest for her!
She was devastated on her arrival,
    after having donned her finery,
After carefully tending her hair
    and using the last of her Channel '95,
He was not there, creating a deep emptiness, a clutching for air.
She had faced calamities before, but this was crushing!
It started with a slight sniffle,
    then a convulsion trying to hold back;
The sobbing uncontrolled as she raced to the storeroom;
Then the staccato of blubbering, moaning and bawling:
She wanted to injure herself, she wanted to end it all,
Then someone realized her problem and said,
"He is ill! He has been for several days!"
Her facial expression changed immediately,
    streaked with tears,
Mascara lined both cheeks as though a painted warrior,
Her entire demeanor changed to one of deep concern.
Grabbing the lapels of the informer, she asked about
His well-being, while unintentionally lifting him off the floor.
Now, her only concern was his welfare,
Gone the self pity, gone the sorrow of selfishness;
Now the only spark and reason for life was,
His existence, his health, his approval of her and her actions.
Gone the discontent, the dismalness;
No longer disheartened, no longer was life cruel.
She had a need, a desire, a goal, a concern for his life.
Only his health mattered, only his welfare.
Rushing out of the door, clothes in hand, she stopped,
Turned in the swirling snow and asked,
"Where does he live?"
And as she stood in the snow with a bewildered look,
A startled look of apprehension, nobody knew!

His Garden Of Life

In his garden of life, there are furrows
Carefully tended and free of weeds,
These furrows contain many plantings
Nurtured by service to others needs.

Nourishment is always available
In the form of tender, loving years,
Moisture is constantly provided
Through his sweat and sometimes tears.

This garden is filled with more than furrows,
It also contains a forest of trees,
Apple, walnut, chestnut and oak are a few
That give shelter from the sun and breeze.

There are ash, maple and locus supplied,
And 'bout some I can't pronounce, he does rave,
As he lovingly touches and smells them
When he removes them fresh from his lathe.

For these represent life's challenges
And the variety of people he meets,
No one is denied at his table;
Philosophical concerns are what you eat.

Now this Garden of Life's not to one place confined,
It's widely maintained without any baulk,
Right now it extends from the southern clime
To Alaska and Vermont and New York!

In a walk through the garden you'll see,
Some vines that hang down like drapes,
These represent energy for life's pruning,
As you partake in the 'juice of the grape'!

There is nothing wasted in this garden of life,
Whether peelings, or fruit from old logs;
It contributes to joy and happiness and love,
For it supplies to the 'roast of the hog'!

So this garden of life is a meeting place
Where ideas and love are of high rank,
And for all his years morality prevailed
In this integrity garden by Frank

Autumn Years

I sat today and reminisced
   Of bygone days of splendor;
T' was initiated by a scene
   That only autumn-time can render.

It reminded me of a life
   In all its joy and glory,
Of decisiveness, of intellect,
   Of an ear for another's story.

Flowers grew throughout the house
   Responding to the gentle care,
Soothing blossoms GRACED the rooms
   Reflecting sunshine everywhere.

And outside mixed aromas
   The gardens do release,
While the pollinating crews
   Hum in idyllic peace.

All this is just a moment
   As I viewed the lakefront scene,
I recalled the vibrant person
   Who lived a life supreme.

Giving love and sage advice,
   Enticing you to think;
The only way to solve your problem
   Was o'er a nice hot drink.

So the memories do linger,
   I'm rejoicing through and through,
And I'm thankful for the privilege
   Of this memory time with you.

I'm Ninety-Nine

I'm Ninety-nine,
On earth I've served my time,
The best thing is, I've kept my mind!
Oh, I knew I was going,
I knew my time had come,
But where I was going,
That's the question asked by some.
Who really cares about that destination,
If you've run the gauntlet true;
If you've lived your life with determination,
It won't matter what's in store for you.
Sure, I was stubborn at times,
Sure, I was formidable and demanding,
Some say toward frugality I was inclined,
But I earned that right, I was understanding.
I kept saying I was ready to depart,
Don't know why there's a pacemaker in my heart,
If my heart stops, do I need a jump-start?
And this abdominal pain is like a dart.
Another thing, when my time has come,
There'll be no longer pain or rage,
If there is a world after this hectic run,
Will I exist as my current self or a dazzling maid?
Nope! None of the above pertain.
Thinking this way is quite insane.
I'll be reborn as an energy burst,
In the heavens, racing across the universe.
At ninety-nine plus a month or two,
I did pretty well, better than many of you.
My one regret is I'd like to see how you react,
When you're ninety-nine with pain in your back.
Fair-thee-well good friends, I love you all,
If there is another place, I'll give you all a call!

The Answers Of A Star

Look! In the heavens! Is there a new star shining there?
When I looked last night
   I didn't see that diamond bright and fair!
I was compelled to gaze,
Transfixed by its luminous and intensive rays.
So irresistible. I watched throughout the night;
It seemed to sink and then hover 'ore the bay,
As a mast-light atop a ship at anchor
   in its safe harbor there afloat.
Then I reflected of what I'd witnessed over the years,
   and thought, not a boat,
But rather a sea plane gliding to a landing safe and sound,
   amidst some ocean spray—
And I wondered where the ship or boat had been, and what
   goodness did it inspire?
With its radiance, did it serve as a beacon for others?
Had it traveled bearing gifts of unselfishness?
On its course, did it display the art of helpfulness?
Was it emulated for its serving so as to right a wrong?
Did it leave the impression that it needed no thanks or reward
   For unasked help in accomplishing another's task?
Did it have a "just go do it" philosophy,
completing the unsavory jobs
   Without complaint, those tasks no one else wanted to do?
In its wake, were there waving hands and tipping hats,
in salutes of thanks that said, "Come back again"?
Then my imagination began to flood with visions,
   Of hardships overcome,
   Of anguish unsurpassed,
Just too complex to render here;
Thoughts, entailing Love, and Peace and War,
And how this star that shines, responded, and took the three,
Love, Peace, and War,

Deep within, to its core;
There within, it let them abide, entwine, and fuse.
Until they were reborn as a new light,
Starting as a radiant glimmer, then an unabashed glow,
Reflecting life, and the living into
"Forgiveness and Freedom to All"
In its eudaemonistic flow. A STAR!

The Departure

The soft snow of early morning
   Clings to trees and grass and stone.
Silently it changed the landscape,
   The black trees no longer a dreary tone.

Bending the grass and shrubs
   As though bowing to the Spirit of Life,
Kneeling before it as THAT essence,
   Changing darkness to purity of white.

Look how it descends, masking every imperfection,
   Listen to the silence, not a leaf rustles nor tree sways,
See the dismalness of the forest change to a hazy
   Majestic splendor with the light of day.

She passed this way spreading charm, leaving
   Her inner beauty behind as was her right,
The Pneuma, the name used by the Greeks,
   So vital and necessary to the strong, or slight.

Yes, she passed this way on her departure,
   From in our midst, from out love and trust;
From her gnarled hands she spread the snow flakes
   As pixies (tinker-bell) sprinkle star-dust.

Leaving behind a scene clean and picturesque
   Remembrance of a new start so intensely bright!
A chance to spiritually and mentally begin afresh;,
   Step out into the crisp noiseless morning white.

And in that stillness hear the call
   To spiritually rise above the petty games,
Start over; revive that spirit of Nature,
   The sources of energies without names.

A white mantle, shinning with no breeze,
   Just a spirit passing over, covering all;
Leaving behind a new look, masking evil,
   Showing that there is a way to answer the call.

A way that culminates in that urge
   To spread goodness and blessings from above,
One Gesture of thanks to all, I'M LEAVIING!
   But in my stead I give you purity and Love!

A new chance to start with good thoughts
   New ideas, new outlooks, true forgiveness, so ring the Bell!
With a revival of faith and trust in each other,
   I leave my Pneuma, use it well.

And I Remembered

Two gulls soared high on updrafts of heated air
   Calling to each other in their tandem flight
   And I remembered my own tandem flights.
The cold ice and snow gave off a mist as
   The warm sun heated the air to give them lift
   And I remembered soaring on updrafts.
I listened as a plane climbed with a serge of power giving
   Thrust to a successful semi-imitation of the gulls
   And I remembered the feel of power, of flight.
The motor droned as the plane increased in altitude
   The pitch changed indicating attainment of a safe height,
   And I remembered.
The breeze wafted the grass above the snow and musically
   entwined and bent the branches of the pine,
The boat sits and patiently waits the
   Arrival of a spring launch and its pilot
   And I remembered with a forlorn look of regret.
Surging through my tortured mind are
   A multitude of memories and regrets;
   Of things I'd wished I'd said and done—
   And I remembered . . . too late!
As I stand outside my home preparing to visit
   The family of one of my very few true friends
   I rest in the secure knowledge that all is not
     lost if the memories are happy and humorous.
   I find that no matter where I look
     Or what I hear, it is a recall of a special moment
     With a friend—-THAT I remember.
Bosom buddies need not communicate . . . they
   Rest in the knowledge that the other is there;
   No words need to be exchanged
   No letters need to be written
   No explanation need be given-
   There is an inner thought, an idea

That is there in a look, or smile,
Or the raising of an eyebrow-
And I remember . . . .
   Silence spoke more to each of us
      For we understood that silence,
      Anticipating each others needs
      Before the need was realized . . .
He wasn't perfect and was a taskmaster
   To those who were too set in their ways
   As he sometimes was in his . . .
And many a harsh word or comment
   Could have been avoided if they could
   Have seen through the veneer
      And not misinterpreted his actions and verbalizations,
   Yes, I remember.
I looked up as a small voice arose from the quietness-
   A fine youth, perhaps too young to truly understand the Alpha and Omega,
   But, I remembered.
His hands knew hard work and blisters, a reality on the road of life;
   Unsheltered from the cold
   Unsheltered from the wind
   Unsheltered from the sleet and rain
   Unsheltered from the fog . . . .
A charted course with complete trust in his compass
   Usually brought him to his destination.
He stood with hammer and saw
   Or his hand upon the tiller or wheel
   Undaunted by what others said and did
He sailed on not searching for the sheltered storm free havens
   But braced against the elements he'd take his choice, saying
      Don't shed too many tears for me
      I lived as well as any could you see
      Do something for others in need
      If you want to really remember me . . . .

Heavenly Bound

Now I'm dancing with Jim and some wine,
Hope I didn't disappoint you by taking my time;
You see, something happened and screwed up my mind,
So my body couldn't reason or rhyme . . . .
I am travelling in this heavenly afterglow,
So look up and you'll see my starry show,
And in that midst, a sudden flash, my halo!
The music send-off continues here
And we are dancing in high gear,
Jim's reception was one to endear,
Beethoven, Brahms, the best, so clear . . .
Jesus himself brought the wine to me,
He really wanted to talk, you see,
And tell me that life was a well-done deed,
He encouraged me and said, "Have no fear".
All the ones I hold so dear
Would join me in some distant years
In the meantime I'm free of tears . . .
Another wonderful goal attained,
I'm singing, playing and using my brain!

Sail On

Sail on, sail on, sail on,
   Oh, ship so sure and fit,
Sail on from this cold darkness
   To a place that's better lit.

I leave behind this tumult
   And the murkiness of strife,
I leave behind dank scheming
   To the planners in the night.

For me it's glorious freedom bells
   Where ever I may roam,
No more uncharted windswept swells,
   As I trim now to the foam.

There on the far horizon,
   A brighter bark I see,
Is that the Kingdom Banner
   From the masthead flying free?

That ship is one we look to
   As a beacon or channel guide;
And we sail the ship in safety
   With dignity and pride.

I see, at last, the source
   Of the guiding, brilliant Grail;
The Navigator of that bark
   Beckons me to trim the sail.

I trimmed the sail with smartness,
   The sheet I released with vision;
Death's not such total darkness,
   Just the images of the living.

So sail on, sail on, sail on,
  Oh, ship so sure and fit,
I've met the Master Mariner,
  With whom I'll stay a bit.

So friends I've left behind,
  Perhaps an enemy or two,
When you decide to change your clime,
  We'll be waiting here for you.

When eventide comes, as it will,
  And darkness seems so near,
Fear not, sing softly and look up,
  There's a bright star shining clear.

Trust that star, because it is
  The topsail of That Bark,
Follow its course and you will see
  On through the pending dark.

Sail on, sail on, oh loved ones,
  Steer for that mighty star,
And I'll be waiting for you,
  In my SHANGRI LA

ALTERNATIVE ENDING

Sail on, sail on, oh anxious one,
  In your ship so sure and fit,
You'll meet the Master mariner,
  With whom you'll stay a bit.

The Guiding Hand

You reached out to take my hand,
  I held back for I didn't feel
    that great to personally touch
The hand of God:
Not while a human on this sod.
As I reached into your hand to follow you,
With my other I reached back for
    a friend or two;
And invited them to follow me
    on a tough rough trail that leads to thee.—
And all my life I've clung to the wheel
    and weathered the storms of truth and zeal
In preference to the serene bay of dishonesty,
    and the complacent channel of "let-it-be".
So accustomed to the reefs of good, sand bars of
    love, and low tide shoals of help I've become,
That those hazards are beacons to the ship of life
    that I command beneath the storm hidden sun;
They let me safely lead my crew to your hand
    in the sheltered harbor of reason,
You gave me the brain and choice and skills
    to do this in any season . . . .
I've made my way by your celestial charts
    through tumultuous currents of deceit,
And although I may not have stilled the raucous
    cries that complacent committees of 'pseudoness' bleat,
It was not because I didn't try,
It was not because I was afraid to stand alone,
It was not because I didn't speak
    or let myself be known—-.
Now, when you reach out to take my hand, I'm tired.
And I don't know if I have the grasp to hold
The hand of God;
Not while a human on this sod . . . .

As you take my hand to be with you,
    did I fulfill my task and reach back
        and grasp the hands of others too?
Tell me God—Did I succeed in being all
    that I could be?
Did I set the example you set for me?
Tell me God—Tell me soon—. . . .
Is that your protective arm about my ship
    of life?
Is that your hand upon the wheel steering
    through this sea of strife?
As I gaze out from this battered bark
    with its scars from uncharted seas,-
I look behind, there in the foaming wake,
Are there a few who are following me?
Reach out as you reached out and took my hand;
Reach out and guide them in their stand—
Give them a glimpse of happiness profound.
    Let them clasp the hand that leadeth me
In your charted course so deep and sound.
Let them weather the storms of sorts,
    and safely bring their ships of life to port.
Although I was once reluctant to take that
    hand extended to take mine,
    I know that now is the proper time—
I now freely reach to personally touch
The hand of God;
Yes, while a human on this sod.
I reach out into your hand to go with you,
And with my other I reach back as a guide
    for a friend or two—
And invite them to chance the course and
    lead some ships for me,
  On a tough rough trail that leads to thee.

Volunteers

Suddenly there sounds the alarm of dread
A fire is the call, the alarm quickly spreads;
From all walks of life they answer the need,
Total devotion is the code of this breed.
They care not if others think they are brave,
The response is volunteer, it's a life they can save!
Cold is the night, darkness increases the chill;
They enter the unknown relying on skill.
Hoses, masks, air packs and lights,
Together they advance, teamwork is tight.
Kick down that door! In we must go!
Though kicking could cause a broken toe!
Methodically some search while others do spray,
Hooks, open ceilings, vent, quick! No delay!
Then comes the call for the fire marshal to start;
Examining the remains, was it caused by a spark?
This activity on a night cold and numb,
Was smoothly enacted because of practice they'd done.
And silently in the rear is a stand-by crew,
No glory bestowed on these stalwart few;
And everyone prays their skills not to test,
Hoping they'll return alone, they're called E.M.S.

Mrs. Pafford's Secret Love

If you met her, you'd think she was demure;
If you knew her, you wouldn't be so sure.
She was aristocratic, almost above reproach;
Opinionated, some subjects she wouldn't broach.
Wealth and position gave her a certain air,
She was demanding, directive, but usually fair.
Certain trails she'd truck along, just for fun;
She was most lady-like, until she shot her gun!
Seeing her take that stance, so sure, so inspired,
When she lifted up that rifle and at the target fired!
Not many knew her love of this precise sport,
No balk, no flinch at the deafening report.
Her eye was keen, her concentration sharp;
'Twas her secret, her love of practice from the start.
When the session was done, guns cleaned and oiled,
She returned again to the formal, the spoiled.
Few knew her as a formidable woman with a rifle;
Now you know, she wasn't one with whom you'd trifle!

Dan E. Blackstone

This Is My Life

Don't tell me how to run my life-
   many have already tried:
And I followed their advice with duty bound allegiance
   but it choked me till I cried.

My spirit won't allow any regimented strife-
   it churns within and suppresses feelings,
Until my mind and body scream for release
   and I cannot face drudgery of daily dealings.

Let me live a less complex existence in my fife-
   and be free to render unto man:
Should the opportunity arise to face a challenge,
   I only ask for strength to make that stand.

The world needs to experience feeling precise-
   for those whose lips produce a sigh
With tormented thoughts to accept the differences
   and let the world go passing by.

Away with your demanding Price!
   it took time to learn that I can
   live my life at my pace,
And not compete or adjust to mankind's
   endless torturous race!

I am who I am in this short spanned life;
   needless is the demanding dogmatic source
Diverting us to accept unreasonable requests
   that could be lifted to the cross!

Let me adopt an old and varied song,
  "Feelings are neither right or wrong",
But an honest expression of who are,
  or want to be
Not copies of what the world wants or
  desires to see!

Place not your unsolved problems in my life,
  or barricade my own straight path:
Rather let me freely walk natures trail
  and greet you there with hardy laugh.

This is me. This is my life:
  Freedom is the road of truth,
And independence leads to caring, agape' love-
  I know because my name is Truus.

Alternate ending:

This is me. This is my life:
  Freedom is all I ever asked
And independence a constant strife-
  This has been my lifelong task.
Now it's done and over, the bell does ring
  Remember me for what I might have been.

Gotta Go 'N Sail

I don't know how it happened,
  But I know it's very true,
There's a beautiful child awaitin'
  An' she's feelin' kinda blue.

Her body is responding
  To a sort of crazy thing,
It's jumpin' an reactin'
  She doesn't even sing.

Brave is this little girl
  An' intelligent to boot,
For that little bug inside,
  She doesn't give uh hoot.

She's gornna bounce right back;
  Scram little bugger, outa my body fair
Scat, you're not welcome in this sack;
  This is MY temple rare.

I've too much ta do,
  My body can't be frail,
Because, by God, this summer,
  I've gotta go 'n sail!

England To New York

From England's shores and chalky clime,
A family excitedly on a ship did climb.
The great day had finally arrived,
To the new world, to a life glorified.
But wild stories did the crew relay,
Caused her a great deal of dismay!
Of how cooking utensils of all types
Were dearly sort for cooking delights!
She being of an industrious clan,
Went back for more pots and pans.
But then to her startled dismay,
The ship set sail that very day!
Alone she stood on the shore with packs,
Yelling for the ship to please come back—
Quickly she rushed to the ships office site
Telling them of her unexpected plight.
Immediately they did secure a single berth
But t'would be a week for the first.
Anguish and crying by children and man,
As they looked to shore where she did stand-
Would this be the beginning of a life of strife?
A devastating feeling of leaving a wife!
No mercy by the crew was ever shown,
As he looked to where she stood alone.
Onward they sailed into the distant foam,
Now over the bounding main they'd roam.
Then they huddled, dark clouds did form
On the horizon, a beastly storm!
For a week and a day it relentlessly blew
Till finally off course they were dashed and askew.
Meanwhile, she trying her best,
On the deck of a ship, looked to the West.
Then wondered how her family would be found
Could they be waiting there safe and sound?

The month did past, then a wonderful sight,
Land HO! We'll be there tonight.
She readied her gear, pots and pans galore,
She'd have them stacked when she reached the shore.
But to her bewilderment and shocking dismay,
His ship didn't arrive before this day!
Then on the horizon sails were seen,
An announcement in a harbor master's scream.
Her family down the gangplank did come
Then seeing her, they screamingly did run!
Their story was told for many years,
Each time t'was done through joyful tears.
How fortunate for them to be enriched this way,
To end up together, in Williamsport P.A.

Philosophy

THEY DIDN'T DIE

They didn't die,
They merely gave up their bodies ...
They live on, and on.
Memories replace the terrestrial forms,
Memories live on and on;
They left this realm, this temporary existence.
From where did we come?
To where do we travel?
For what were we preparing while here?
This transitional phase we call LIFE,
To what purpose?
Is it to experience pain and love
to better allow us to enter a new realm?
With all the struggles and joys that exist,
Must we learn these,
   to prepare us for forthcoming situation
   for which we must cope so as to better
   help those in need ... ?
Are we on a trip and periodically rest for
Rejuvenation and learning so as to enable others?
Are we tested and educated in the
Worldly ways, then sent back in time
To serve others and help the less fortunate,
Help prepare them for earth?
Then, pass on to another existence,
A new plateau, where we again
Are the students, learning patience and
Strengthening ourselves for the ultimate
Meeting with the power of the universe!
How many steps are there to attain the ultimate level?
Instituted by the attainment of what resembles Brahmanism,
Buddhism, Taoism, Shinto-ism, ...
Did they have the incite during their heyday?
Are their stone stele, Stupah, Temples, Tori,
What others brought back, or forward from prior existence?

From the future or the past?
Are the strange findings, discoveries,
Unexplained buried objects,
Clues of passing through this existence
to the future, or past, but always
Leaving the bodies and re-entering new
Forms of existence, the embodiment of
Endless life, that goes on and on
Just in a different form

A Leader

Years have passed since that infamous day
When suddenly a helmsman was called away:
He answered the summons of his eternal guide
And reluctantly left his loved one's sides,
To continue his work in another realm
On a greater ship he took the helm:
Reserving space for those who may follow
Through channels deep or even shallow.
We do not know our ultimate fate,
A rich, or a high, or a lowly state;
But if in our hearts and in our minds,
We seek the "points" he left behind,
Then we'll navigate true and trim
Till finally we are at one with HIM.

ANCESTORS

I thought of my ancestors today,
And wondered how their parents felt
When they kissed and hugged farewell,
Never to return to where their parents dwelt.
Grandmother Annie Maria especially comes to mind,
From the rural mountains of Tyrol roots,
The Grossglockner Glacier far above
The beautiful village of Heiligeblut.
Did she have a tearful trip to the unknown?
Or was it a trip of wild anticipation?
Shedding old memories of hardships and despair,
Or recalling gaiety and joyous celebrations?
But I wonder, when she held me and rocked me,
In the chair from her grandmother's farm,
Did she think then of her grandmother's loving embrace,
Did she mentally transcend me to maternal arms?
I'll never know, because she died in 49 days of my birth,
Did she yodel in her melodious Austrian trill?
As I may have gurgled looking with inquiring eyes?
Did I respond with smile to give her a thrill?
There is no way to really tell,
For I was the only grandchild she ever held.
And all the ones who could answer my quest,
Have also been gently laid to rest.

Eddie's Sweet Shop

The outside appearance belied the neat interior.
The sight of mouth watering candy was superior,
Opening the door you were wafted by delectable smells.
Everyone who entered was captivated by odiferous spells.
And ice cream sundaes with the cream freshly churned,
Accompanied by cherries atop whipped cream less firm,
Was ordered by high school students crowding the booths,
Cared not what the dentist claimed it would do to a tooth!
And drinks were ordered in an ice filled glass
Not served in a bottle, this place had class;
So cold that one could suffer from brain freeze,
To wash down the sandwiches of real grilled cheese
But the candy, homemade, with real sugar and spice,
Displayed in a case designed to entice,
Was protected with a curved glass front,
As in your mouth there formed a watery lump.
People came from all over to sit, talk and eat,
Anyone seeing you walking down the street,
With a cone or takeout knew of your stop.
You had just visited Eddie's Sweet Shop . . .
(The Best New Britain Candy And Ice Cream Stop.)

I May Not Be

I may not be a leader,
And yet, I'm not really a follower-
I am me, independent—a part of the whole,
But an important part:
I submit when submissiveness is
   required for kindness and uplifting,
I rebel when it is in the cause
   of righteousness, to quell the unjust-
There is no misunderstanding in
   the striving for peace of mind;
It is setting the example, a living
   example for others to emulate.
It leads to a loving peace,
A peace that awakens the inner love,
   a submissive love,
Yet a strengthening love:
In my mind I am clear on this,
So I may not be a leader,
And not really a follower-
Just an example setter,
The same as you.
Not retaliatory, but forgiving,
Not belittling, but uplifting,
Not demeaning, but supportive,
So you see, we agree in principle.
If you think of me as a leader, don't.
I merely went my way,
  The way that emphasized life-
    The living,
    The beauty,
    Nature,
For nature is life,
A personification of goodness.

Two Shadows

Two shadows formed as I walked along
Beginning in the unfolding of a brand new dawn.
One I know was mine
But the other? Was it thine?
Was it my other self? My other living?
The one that is reasonable and forgiving?
Are there two such shadows to every human being?
Are there two souls and one is never seen?
Who can say or positively claim with zeal
That there in the unseen is a guardian that's real
Whether that other shadow is our inner soul
Clinging as an aura enveloping love untold
Or just an external mask standing aloof
Presenting to others our longing for truth.
Two shadows as I walk along
They grow and cross as a cadence of song
Two shadows in the early Pre-sunrise
They disappear and then rematerialize
They begin as one and suddenly there are two
One is me—the other is who?
They keep me company on my predawn stroll
It mystifies me as my legs pay the toll.
And my mind plays tricks envisioning an unseen friend
Who leads and guides to our life's end;
Who tries to influence our predestined lives'
Who loves and cherishes our deeds and lies,
That we may make to defend our deeds.
Whether to ourselves or others of our seeds.

Labor Day 2002

Labor day, a day of family gatherings
The hustle bustle of activities and planning's,
A time when siblings organize for the older folk,
To repay them for the years when they were broke;
You bring the salad, you the chicken breasts-
You the hot dogs and what goes with 'em best.
The hamburgers, rolls and potato chips
Along with desserts and exotic dips,
Can be furnished by the offering host
In a place designed to "fit the most".
When the grandparents come to visit there
Be sure to tell kids they can't touch the fare!
But let them know it's for a "family picnic Saturday",
Not for the grandfather's diamond jubilee birthday!!!
And mention to them that they should not speak too much
Like saying,' it is for you know what!!'
Or whisper in too loud a voice or go and say
"Don't touch that, it's for Papa's day!"
Or keep the excitement out as voices rise,
How on Saturday there'll be a big surprise!
It's part of growing with the territory
As kids mature in all their glory!
And grandparents have only one chance
To reach an age that's "in advance,"
And still be able to sing and quote
To youngsters on whom they dote!
So keep the spirit, laugh and bray,
And party every LABOR DAY!

Follow Me

Follow me, I'll lead you through,
Follow me, I'll guide your way;
Through the forest or deserts bare,
Follow me, I'll be there!

Over mountains ever so high,
Some reaching through clouds to the blue sky.
Enter valleys, along streams so swift,
Or past alpine lakes and deep wide rifts.

Follow me, trust me, know I'll be there,
Let me lead and show the way,
Use your mind, be pure of heart,
So you'll be able to lead one day.

Greet all you meet with your smile serene,
Comfort others on your adventure trail;
Follow me, I'll lead you to a new scene,
And the world will smile at hill and dale.

Now's your turn to shout with glee,
I'll lead you through so follow me,
The one I followed led me well,
And the call resounds clear as a bell,
Follow me, follow me, follow me.

For Tia, my covergirl

Sandy

A memorable all Saints day,
   After October, two thousand and Twelve,
When darkness descended
   And the Oceans did swell.

But prior to this time-
   Of agony and destruction,
Was the memory of Sandy,
   One of pleasant seduction.

There's the Sandy with Annie,
   The life saving mutt,
And Daddy Warbucks of
   Wealth and such . . .

There are Sandy beaches
   That stretch for miles
With semi-clad women
   And seductive smiles.

The Sandy of old,
   Meant no damage or wreck,
"Twas neither blonde nor redhead,
Or even brunette.

An attractive maiden
   With an ageless face,
All dressed for pleasure,
   In gloves and lace.

Then there's the Sandy
   Of dry dessert fame,
Where Lawrence did ride
   So they wildly claim.

The Sandy of color
   the nice shade of tan,
That often is gotten
   To look alluring on sand.

There are Sandy Banks
   Of glacial deposits
And sand hidden deep
   In some dusty closets.

Remember also whether
   Cold or warm,
Occasionally we cope
   With a Sandy Storm.

Forget you not
   Houses built on land Sandy
Often collapse
   Leaving one angry.

Snow on roads,
   Are sometimes Sandy,
Making driving,
   Safe with scenes so dandy.

So look upon Sandy
   With a different view,
Pleasant or unpleasant,
   Depends upon you.

The Spirit of Progress

She stands above the community, day or night,
Once completely enshrouded in glowing white;
Against a background of opulent green,
Balanced on a sphere, so delicate, so keen.

Carrying a torch to lead the world, day or night,
To those in peril, need or in flight:
Tip toeing onward, a vision serene
Bringing relief, full-filling a dream.

She is a Spirit, no longer followed by day or night,
But now forgotten, this dedicated angelic sight,
Her redeeming qualities no longer reign supreme,
The caduceus only leads, she trails, losing steam.

Now she is decaying, alone both day and night'
Her majestic pose ignored, forgotten is her plight.
Above her the protective arch decays, piece by piece;
Still she Nobly stands, a protector of the weak.

And below, ignoring her both day and night,
They blithely pass, no thought of her statuesque might:
Till she falls one day, onto the Artistic Egress,
This formidable female, This Spirit of Progress.

This is the facade above the new location of the Art Center in Westerly.

Do I Have To Be Free

Do I have to be free?
What does it mean when I say I'm free?
My color isn't black
My color isn't white
My color isn't in between
My color is Free!
I have my rights! is the scream!
Who gave those rights?
Do I have to roam at will?
Who gave me the right to say I'm Free?
Do I have the right to dream,
Is my life controlled by another's scheme

NO. no no—I don't have to be free-
This isn't a gift- it isn't a right!
Someone sacrificed with all their might,
So as to let me stand in a mountain breeze
Inhale while 'ore looking the sea of trees
With expanded lungs and a AHH exhalation,
I rejoice and smile in great supplication
My mind is exhilarated with multiple distractions
I've climbed and observed with great satisfaction.
Below I can trace the reflecting white ribbons
Which earlier I had splashed across with mixed visions.

Unsurpassed Christian

Quiet, unassuming, an independent thinker;
A person with a quick smile, and bright eyes,
Who is ready to render aid on a moment's notice
To those with lesser abilities and greater needs.
A recluse, yet available to communicate,
Communicate in an articulate manner with logic.
A person who is of mild manner and respect;
Powerfully built, physically capable and
Trained as a combatant, but mercifully understanding.
A person who avoids confrontation rather than argue-
This person supports the community without them knowing!
One church benefits greatly, although the person is not an active participant.
This kind of support has been rendered over the years.
The pain he uncomplainingly endured is only now
Visibly becoming obvious in restricted activities.
There are many such persons who go un-rewarded.
This person's name is anonymous and will likely
Pass into oblivion unless you become, in the immortal
Words of HARRY POTTER, a seeker.

Remembrance

Solemnly we sit, solemnly we wait,
He lies there not noticing anyone,
He lies there not conscious of the date.

So quietly we whisper, silently we weep;
He lies there, a valiant son,
They tip-toe so as not to disturb his sleep.

A voice breaks the silence, then an ensuing hush,
She reverently spoke of this virtuous one,
She spoke not of admirable accolades robust!

This free spirit person had his own will,
Didn't dwell on things he'd done,
Just did what was needed, seeking not any thrill.

He's remembered for no great individual cause,
Many know of how children thought him lots of fun,
He incited them because he played Santa Claus!

Sleep well now, she continued to say, sleep in peace,
Rest from the cognitive life from which you did run,
You answered the freedom call, contentment now will never cease.

Look Deeply

Look deeply into my eyes and tell me what you see;
Are they deep and penetrating pools of love?
Do they reflect the hidden emotions of concern?
Can you see the conflagration of compassion,
Waiting to be released and combine with a
Kindred soul?
Unless you look beyond the blemished face,
Or the wrinkles of concentration and thought,
Unless you look beyond the pallor, the color of
Ones skin,
You will not witness the smile, the purity of
Heart,
Nor be enveloped in the sunshine hidden there.
Enter into me, look deeply into my eyes and tell me What you see.
I welcome you to search for that inner me,
And become entwined with thoughts, relinquished Through exposing
barriers that you inadvertently Think Are there.
And tear them down so that we may indulge,
Intermingle
In common camaraderie of trust, unconditional Undeniable support,
And faith in each other.
If you look deeply into my eyes and do not see
My need of you,
Not see my dreams,
Not see my sunshine,
Not see my agape` love,
Then you do not see me,
And you do nothing to release the light therein.

Dan E. Blackstone

Sunset of The Season

Most people think of Seasons as a certain time of year;
They mark comfort levels of people and their careers.
Seasons mark the times when you can play out in the sun,
Or ski, or swim, or pile the leaves just for jumping fun.
Seasons also mark the renewing of a garden life,
You plant the seeds, nurture, pulling all the weeds on sight!
Then carefully you spray for any invading hoard,
Some look pretty, very fancy but that is just a fraud.
Identifying them is certainly a constant full time job,
This is training to recognize the pests that truly rob!
They'll devastate the crops if allowed to be freed,
There's a chemical equation, so they cannot go and breed.
Then the season that is best, the one at harvest time,
A few of the Tomatoes, huge, are still upon the vine.
You pick them, almost bursting, a fruit that once was green;
And slice them and prepare them for a meal that's so supreme!
Seasons all come to an end, just as humans must also do,
The seasons of one's life depends upon your point of view:
Different ages of your life are seasons in the Natural Realm,
You steer your season-ship, with your strong hand on the helm!
Infancy, a season of wonderment, a winter, can't wait for it to end,
Youth, a season of transition, curiosity is the trend;
Adolescence, a season for maturity, tending the planted seeds.
Young adult, a season to experiment, the removing of the weeds:
Adulthood, a season for caring for the whole garden plot,
Middle age, the season of surprises, supervising the striving lot.
Then old age, a season of reflection, revisiting the past
Wondering what happened, the gracious living went so fast!
Yes, life's full of many seasons, each continues to an end,
If you can reflect upon a life of Joy, then the 'Sunset of the Seasons' is a friend!.

Inspired by Ron Careb mentioning the Sunset of the Seasons as a Statement made by his parents.

STONINGTON STROLL

Friday, December third, cold and dank;
Overcast skies, slight breezes chill you to the bone,
But spirits are bright, friends stroll in rank-
Smiles, voices raised on high as through the village they roam.

At the Park, they start with resounding song so merry-
Youngsters mill, or hold a warm hand reassuring,
Then start the people from the green, no tarry!
Roads are closed, a street walk so alluring.

Off key or on key, it makes no difference;
Join in the spirit, sing out loud and strong,
It matters not, sing as through a child's innocence;
All notes are good notes, no notes are wrong.

The venders have opened their doors this night,
Open doors line the whole street,
To show their wares and serve you a delightful bite.
(Some foods exotic, some foods are sweet)

Then community unites and burst forth in song,
Content to know that we are all together,
Now the season is here to celebrate in throngs,
The season to love, be it that way forever;

There is nothing more inviting on December the three
Than the love shown through singing, whether warm or cold,
Love and Peace and Music, these three,
Are always in vogue on the Stonington Stroll.

Sitting in car at United Church . . . . Mileage 122221

Dan E. Blackstone

What's There To Complain About . . .

I've stood upon the mountain tops
And reached up towards the sky;
I've climbed upon glaciers white,
Where the glare would hurt your eyes!
Then there were the desert trips,
Where the sand was hot and dry;
And I've sailed upon the oceans blue,
Where the water meets the sky-
In between the trails have led
To people with smiles and pride;
Some were happy that we came,
Some so glad they cried!
That made me proud to see,
In each place Love abides.
Out on the trails where Nature lives,
There nothing needs to hide;
We are all one with red blood
That pulsates deep inside-
So enjoy your travels in this life,
Let curiosity be your guide
And you'll live life to the fullest,
With a mind well satisfied.

Valentines

A Moment

There's moment in every day
When you stop and think and rest
While you calculate life's position
And the many ways you're blest.

As a man there's much to be desired
Even though I think I've seen the light
In your presence I was inspired
There were times I'd rather have been right.

There is no way in which I can revive
The many hours that I've been at fault
O sure, I can wish and plan and strive
But I cannot change that tight locked vault.

'Tis too late to go back into time
To piece together the broken thoughts
To reclaim the missing hours sublime
Too late to mend the feelings wrought.

So again as the hours swish away
And we solemnly sit in this old clime
And look to see the bright light of day
Then I ask, Are you still my Valentine?

Dusting

A duty or an exercise of care?
A task or a home review?
Each item carefully lifted and arranged
    just moved a smidgen to the left or right
    so that it's attractive to ones sight.
There's a phase of mental gymnastics
That goes on with each loving touch,
'would this look better here or there'
With each delicate rub,
    'I wonder how it would look on the other shelf,
    or on the table near the window' says she to self.
And with each careful repositioning
A thought to the origin of the gift
    and the thoughtfulness of someone dear,
    who proved themselves throughout the years.
Though sometimes a wild thought comes to pass
I've too much here!
I think I'll give it to the fair' . . .
    but she never really does, you see,
    cuz it's her home, with memorials dust free.

WHO IS MOST PERFECT

Who is most perfect, a venerable star . . . You are.
Who arranges items for a perfect view . . . You do.
Who ablely cleans things so spic and span . . . you can.
Who keeps records, especially our money . . . you honey.
Who always looks so clean and fine . . . you valentine.

       Will you be mine?

Emeralds

Emeralds are precious stones, formed under pressure
   like diamonds only more beautiful, green-
They are ageless in a time of changeless measure
   reaching and calling you as in a dream.
You may hold them, feel them, even love them,
   but can they comfort you as a sage?
They appear without flaw and without feeling
   while we continue to battle old age.
We in life do not envision ourselves
   as eternally living on as the emerald might;
Yet in love we see others, not as aged, or aging,
   but as we first saw the emerald reflecting light.
There, standing in the solitude, radiantly,
   the sparkle of a thousand points of sun,
Each point a facet mirroring without flaw
   the inner beauty that lives the three in one.
Look how it shines: see how it entwines:
   see how it draws you in and surrounds.
It gives itself without regard for self,
   it knows no limits or earthly bounds.
As in an intimate embrace and trusting touch
   where love can overcome the strife,
The emeralds beauty is limited and its love is such,
   not like the agelessness as within my loving wife.

What's Wrong With Society?

Civility has died! Politeness is buried!
The funerals have been long and consuming.
Common Courtesies have not been introduced,
Never revealed, not manners, nor respect,
Things of the past, during the young
Informative, impressionable years.
Vile language is the challenge overpowering
Pureness of heart-
It's mine, it's me, it's my right, its freedom
Of expression! At who's expense?
And Society will die or is dying.
Rudeness, abusiveness, common public displays;
Sexual intimacy no longer a private, loving array.
Vulgarity, a familiar display taught by parents,
Through emulation in actions and in speech.
Society now allows ill breeding,
Lowering her standards,
To the level of psychotic criminals, ne'er-do-wells.
Excuse me; Pardon me; Let me hold the door:
Please; Thank you; You are welcome,
Are ancient terms unheard by youth today!
It's me, It's mine, it's my way or the highway!
How can a teacher teach values if parents have none?
How can preachers preach truth if parents have none?
Something for nothing is perpetuated,
Insults and derogatory, defaming comments prevail!
Bullying a common practice in the neighborhoods,
Where once any parent would step in and the
Parent of the offending child would thank them!
Law suits due to greed and being ashamed of what was done
Are prevalent and initiated by jealousy.

Notes

Once upon a time
There was a
Little
Note.
At
First
It was an
Eighth note.
Then it became
A quarter note.
Finally it held out till
It became a half note!
Eventually in its entirety
It became a whole note!
A note of completeness,
And in its wholeness
It held on longer
Than any other,
A note of love,
A note of nice
Memories
A note
Of
Unity.
A *whole* note is better than a *half,* which is
Better than a *quarter* which is better than an *eighth.*
The world cannot do without notes;
When combined, or united, they create
Harmony and a symphony of life and peace.
No notes cause unhappiness! When you
First enter an empty home,
You look for a note of harmony—-
No note is dissident and discordant:
The mental ear listens intently to the
Vibrations of such a note—or no note,

When absent, a stillness and deafening
Silence ensues . . . .
So bring joviality and spring to your loves,
Enthrall them with *eighth, quarter, half, whole* notes galore
And there'll be a harmonic and symphonic life of amour . . .

Royale Jelly

Sometimes, Royale Jelly is called Honey!
That's true, not tryin' to be funny;
So if I call you honey, Honey, recall that honey won't spoil!
It means you have a lineage along the lines regally Royale!
And that continues for all eternal time,
So, will you continue to be my Valentine?

love always
dan

Questions

Am I always oblivious to your needs?
Do I never see the undone chores?
I hear you chide others for their thoughtlessness,
And ask myself if as a husband,
   Did I fail your desires?
   Did I inadvertently ignore you?
   Did I abandon your hour of distress?
   Did I become incompetent as your friend?
Did I neglect the things you wanted me
  To do, while I was on a think project?
When and how was I so inept at being
   What you thought I should be?
   What you thought I should think?
   What you thought I should peruse?
   What you thought I should know
      Without being told what it was?
I know I love you, but there is doubt,
   As to why you can't feel it,
   As to why you can't see it,
   As to why I don't say it often enough.
   It is through cards or verbal contact
   That this display is evidenced as unification.
Oblivious? Probably. Deaf? Probably. Inept? Probably.
Blind to your concern? No!
Appreciative to your continuous efforts? Definitely!
Love you? Without question!
Please, be my Valentine . . . .

GRATITUDE

Gratitude is only a word of appreciation,
But it is a word glorifying one of creation;
Describing the indescribable uniqueness and mirth
That descended upon the earth in miracle of your birth.
In that moment joy spread far and near
And untold happiness banished fear,
While the living unknowingly ceased their daily grind,
Preparing you to be my valentine.

WILL YOU BE MINE?

2-14-99,?

Dan E. Blackstone

Each Day I Give Thanks

Each morning I look out of darkness
To the Star and sometimes moonlit grounds.
I need to wake with mental sharpness,
From the needed sleep so sound.
I burst forth giving a silent shout,
Running on silent trails,
I give thanks as the miles do mount,
At times I sing songs, hardy and hale.
The years have passed, but it's still the same,
When I look out at the dawning light
And imagine that I am not lame,
Then look in the face, what a memorable sight!
But I carry deep in my mental cells,
The youthful image of one who has taken time
To cheer me and keeps me well,
She is my only Valentine . . . .

For tomorrow . . . . and all the remaining tomorrows.

Barbe

Haircut

So Sophisticated, so demure, so perfectly coiffeured-
She radiates splendor, resplendently matured,
All respect her, all welcome her, all identify with her;
She, like a kitten, like a dove, her voice more like a purr,
Today she is special, today is divisive, today is more than fair-
For she has spent the day with a friend, who carefully curled her hair.

Come—Walk Along With Me

Come—walk along with me and listen to my song.
We can walk along together, neither ahead nor behind-
For soon we may be parting, for the road's not very long,
And during our brief encounter let's observe every sign,
   of newness, of intellect, of beauty and other thrills,
   of vistas beyond description, of valleys and their hills.
Perhaps we'll traverse mountains
   and cross their tumultuous streams
With the dashing, crashing, smashing,
   and its swirling steam.
We'll listen to the silence in needle-strewn pine groves,
We'll sing our song in joyous laughter
   as we travel on or doze-
We'll watch the birds that soar
   and hear the music of their bills,
Some so soft and melodious, others coarse and shrill.
As long as you are with me and I feel the love we share,
We can stop and smell the flowers or aromas anywhere-
Come, walk along with me and I'll listen to your song,
For soon we may be parting, for the road's not very long.

A Kind Lady

(or they threw away the mold)

Intellectually superior, but not lauding!
Simple encouraging words of speech;
A voracious appetite for the deep and philosophical . . .
Magically these reinforce her searching mind,
An unquenchable thirst for knowledge.

An unending search through the Universe of Thoughts
Challenging the mystique, the Holies, the Gandhi's,
Aristotle, the Eudameans!
Wondering at the words of Buddha, Brahman, I Ching.
Why Jesus? Why God? Who stimulated and initiated
   these writers,
   these leaders,
   these philosophers and to what end? (even Lenin)
Each works in reality can be reduced to one or two words:
   Love!
   Forgive!

Such was her unsatisfied search
   For a way to show others,
   For the need to see good,
   For the quiet response,
     The quiet debate,
     The quiet sharing,
     The acceptance of a contrary point of view . . .

Her mind constantly and boldly settled on these letters of the alphabet:
   The "W"
   The "H"
   The "Y"
And the greatest of these is "Y"!
Her favorite word, "WHY"!

Why do you suppose people act that way?
Why do you suppose they painted their door that color?
These 'Whys' made her wonder so that it developed into
    I wonder why she does that?
    I wonder what that house looks like inside?
    I wonder about the interior of the Old Baptist Church?
    I wonder if . . . .

Her logic was exceptional,
Her ESP was extraordinary,
Many thought they put one over on her . . . . but she knew!
    She felt it,
    She kept it to herself.
I wonder why that man has a limp,
I wonder why that woman tilts her head,
I wonder why I don't like to cook (No, really just threw this in!)

Of her it has been said:
    She is a lady,
    She is very nice,
    She is trustworthy and kind,
    She keeps your secret,
    She exemplifies the teachings of Jesus, a great man!
    She loved Gandhi,
    She loved Music especially La Boehm.
    She lived Music,
    She is:
        a symphony of life,
        a symphony of love,
        a symphony of motherhood,
        a symphonic wife!

If there is a God,
She is an important part of God . . .
Her contributions fortify God . . .
If not, her legacy still remains
    To instill goodness in the lives of humankind!

Dan E. Blackstone

A Rose Among Roses

The birth of a rose is beautiful to watch,
A bud forms with no visual hint or clue
Of what's wrapped in a green cloaked swatch
Protecting an inner breath-taking view.

Then, slowly it develops its own array
Bursting forth it rolls back the green,
And opens itself in a colorful display,
Maturing, disclosing a flower supreme!

You are a Rose, developed carefully in Love;
You transformed into a marvelous state!
Guided by a spiritual Cosmos from above,
Perfection took years, ten times eight!

We are thankful for you, a real nice Lady,
We are thankful for your joy and mirth,
And we celebrate your life, yes at Eighty,
Recalling July 19th, the day of your birth!

Love, dan . . . 2010

BRIDGES

Two cities, two ways,
    Isolated, alone, separated by a stream;
Two people, two thoughts,
    Isolated, alone, separated by distance,
All in need of connections to survive.
The common denominator,
    A BRIDGE.
Over the years, many bridges are crossed,
    Bridges of joy, bridges of sorrow,
But always, bridges of connections to a better life.
    Some bridges are complex,
    Some bridges are simple.
Bridges are created to convey a variety of needs,
Even Mother Nature has her way of crossing barriers.
Let us continue to cross bridges,
    Not alone, not separately, but together.
And, if we find ourselves on opposite sides,
    We'll meet in the middle,
    Or, look down on those bridges
That unite two sides,
    Two cities, two ways
    Two people, Two thoughts,
    No longer isolated, No longer alone,
        Bridged to a better connection,
        Bridged to a better life-
(Thanks for being my bridge
    For fifty-eight years.)

Music Makers

The end of the toilet roll brings joy
As well as the paper towel tube, A Toy!
It serves a mega-phone for some,
Stimulates marching music fun.

Hear the tooting merrily keeping beat,
With kitchen stomping of bare feet!
Giggling ensues and laughter too,
With a pile of paper beneath your shoe!

Spur of the moment after Barbara tooted through
a paper towel tube on her way to the garbage can,
imitating the kids when they were young.

Your Love

Your love creates a flood of waves
That crashes against the resistance of hate;
A spray of forgiveness causes a harmonious rave,
Drowning out jealous storms of deceit, they abate.

Then on the flood of goodness dwells abundant love,
In the act of acceptance, peace radiates in a gold beam';
You are that angelic rain that streams from above,
Overflowing banks, spreading comfort supreme.

A Symphony Of Life

In transition from a budding beauty
To a full young bloom
You've managed your life without
Sadness or gloom.

Each morning with the breaking dawn
As a flower preparing to bloom,
You unfold, deliberately developing
Each duty so as to mature by noon.

Throughout the hours you constantly
And earnestly tend your flock and home
Cleaning and planning and encouraging
Others by visits and by phone.

As evening comes the full bloom
Radiates as you sit to rest,
Knowing you've served, are loved
And done your very best.

You are a symphony of
How others see your life,
Amazing, Encouraging, Emulating
Love and Spiritual delight.

Dan E. Blackstone

At The Flood Of Our Lives

At the flood of our lives
We have an over abundance
Of material needs and treasure
   But this wouldn't exist,
   If you didn't persist,
By sharing your loving as the measure!

At the flood of our lives,
We are abundantly surprised
Of the treasures materialized
   But this wouldn't exist
   If you didn't persist,
In your sharing so caring and personalized.

The water of earth really strives
To support as new births arrive,
'Tis the essence for the saving of lives!
   You extrude that clear fluid of life,
   With each breath to eliminate strife,
As you breathe love into life so alive.

I don't know . . . got carried away trying to
make sense about the most important
Things in life at different stages . . . figured I'd
put it down so as to work on it later
And get rid of the paper stacks.

The Way

The path of life is not always straight
Or smooth, or level, or even shaded.
It's one's attitude that determines how great
A life might be eventually graded.
It leads past quiet pools so calm and clear,
In mountains, valleys, or plains or ridges,
Enhancing your chances to act as a seer,
Helping others to build their bridges.
Small minds, average minds, great minds
All have their place in planning your life;
But you are the leader of times and signs,
And instill discussions in ideas of what's right!
Christian disciples are needed to enter the race
You are willing to enter and run!
With your abilities you accept second place
No need for recognition when you are done!
Many would emulate your loving way,
Being happy to copy your glorious life,
And at seventy seven they'd gratefully say
She is My image of a beautiful sight!

Your Aura

The aura of your soul illuminates your way
There is no possible transgression of ill thoughts pending.
Only a corona of brilliance emitting a kindness display,
Tenderness transmits hate to love through minds transcending.

A person is awakened by your approaching ray,
There is an uplifting in viewing you as "the human race".
And your eyes reflect the inner earnestness of day,
Night removed, elation soars in seeing your radiant face.

Justice for all is emulated from your approaching,
A faith to live by is perpetuated in the ether of others,
In their examination of their own self indulging,
They peel from themselves the masking covers,

Exposing their aura, and baring their souls,
Confessing their inner secrets to your receptive care,
With their burden lifted they adapt a new role;
This is your gift so delightful and so rare.

Look For Me

In the beauty of the sunrise, don't grieve,
For I have lived my life as I saw fit, with no apologies!
Look for me in a breath-taking scene,
Look for me in colorful leaves or flowers.
When you see a walking tree,
Or something strange, think of me . . . .
While walking in canyons steep and colorful,
Reflecting ancient life, think of me:
Or on a snow covered morning so quiet
Look for me, I'll be there!
During a Snowstorm,
In an open field of an old farm,
My spirit will be there.
Look for me in a brook, or pond,,
And in the reflections there,
It will mirror my spirit . . . .
I am not gone, just metamorphosed;
I am now part of every sunrise and sunset.
Rejoice, for I leave you my Pneuma!
The vital spirit of my existence!
Not that I could not be ornery or obstinate at times;
Forgive and forget those moments of insanity!
But still look for me, for generally I have lived
As god saw fit! She led me on!
So I leave my Pneuma to you . . .
Use it well!.

www.ingramcontent.com/pod-product-compliance
Lightning Source LLC
Chambersburg PA
CBHW030113100526
44591CB00009B/391